"Melinda and Kathy have put together  identify and embrace your own personal
refreshing, and a message every mom n

—Jill Savage, founder and CEO of
books, including *No More Perfect Moms*

"I would have benefited from a book like this so many years ago."

—from the foreword by Suzanne (Suzie) Eller,
speaker and author, *The Mom I Want to Be*

"Motherhood is hard no matter what way you slice it! I love the heart
Kathy and Melinda have to encourage and equip mothers to do it well!"

—Jennifer Maggio, chief executive officer of The Life of a Single
Mom Ministries and award-winning author

"Authors Melinda Means and Kathy Helgemo are relatable, practical,
and compassionate. Feed your heart, mind, and soul with the wisdom
found in *Mothering From Scratch*."

—Lori Wildenberg, co-author of three parenting books,
including *Raising Little Kids with Big Love*
and *Raising Big Kids with Supernatural Love*

"Instead of living frustrated from always falling short, Melinda and Kathy
free us into the power of mothering as our truest, God-created self."

—Amy Carroll, Proverbs 31 Ministries speaker and author

"*Mothering From Scratch* helps moms enjoy the journey of their own
personal recipe for parenting and find freedom in knowing that there
are no cookie-cutter families—so there are no cookie-cutter solu-
tions—and that's okay."

—Stephanie Shott, founder of M.O.M. Initiative

"Melinda and Kathy give moms permission to experiment in freedom
from the fear of doing it wrong in order to create a unique parenting
recipe for success. This book is a must-have for every mother."

—Heather R. Riggleman, blogger, speaker, mom, and author of
Mama Needs a Time-Out

"*Mothering From Scratch* offers strategies and stirring questions to
help busy moms fully enjoy all that God has for them."

—Gayle Wright, ministry outreach lead, MOPS International, Inc.

MOTHERING
from Scratch

MOTHERING
from Scratch

Finding the
BEST PARENTING STYLE
for You and Your Family

Melinda Means & Kathy Helgemo

BETHANY HOUSE PUBLISHERS

a division of Baker Publishing Group
Minneapolis, Minnesota

Published by Bethany House Publishers
11400 Hampshire Avenue South
Bloomington, Minnesota 55438
www.bethanyhouse.com

Bethany House Publishers is a division of
Baker Publishing Group, Grand Rapids, Michigan

Printed in the United States of America

Library of Congress Cataloging-in-Publication Data
Means, Melinda.
    Mothering from scratch : finding the best parenting style for you and your family / Melinda Means and Kathleen Helgemo.
        pages cm.
    Includes bibliographical references.
    Summary: "For those who are tired of cookie-cutter parenting approaches, two Christian moms encourage readers to develop flexible, personal mothering styles that work best for their own families"—Provided by publisher.
    ISBN 978-0-7642-1264-2 (pbk. : alk. paper) 1. Motherhood—Religious aspects—Christianity. 2. Parenting—Religious aspects—Christianity. 3. Child rearing—Religious aspects—Christianity. I. Helgemo, Kathleen. II. Title.
BV4529.18.M43 2015
248.8′431—dc23   2014032147

Cover design by Paul Higdon

Authors are represented by The Blythe Daniel Agency.

15 16 17 18 19 20 21   7 6 5 4 3 2 1

From Melinda
To my children, Molly and Micah. I love you very
much and am so grateful for how God has used you
to grow my character and dependence on Him.
I pray that you will always allow Him to
lead your journeys.

From Kathy
To my mom, who mothered me through difficult
times and always silently claimed my life for
God's purpose, not her own. I love you.

Contents

Foreword by Suzanne Eller   11

Acknowledgments   15

Introduction: How Did We Get Here?   17

Section I: Welcome to the Mothering Kitchen

1. New Motherhood Starts With a New Plan   23

2. All Mothers Can Start From Scratch   34

3. What Happens When You Feel Like You're Not a Good Mom?   45

Section II: The Spicy Realities of Motherhood

4. Mothering the Way You're Made   57

5. Claiming Your Identity and Aligning Your Priorities   69

6. Good News: Your Future Won't Spoil   81

Contents

Section III: Sifting It All Out

7. Working With What Your Mama Gave You   97

8. Tasting and Seeing What Is Good   109

9. Mom Mentors: Turning Rivals to
   Resources   121

Section IV: Mothering With Wisdom and Grace

10. Satisfying Self-Care   139

11. Valuing Your Role   152

12. Creating Home   163

13. Feeding Your Soul   177

14. Depending on God's Power 190

Appendix   199

Notes   203

About the Authors   205

Foreword

Years ago when I was a mom to three little ones under the age of two, I was completely certain that anybody could parent better than me.

It's not that I didn't love being a mom. I did! But all of those things that were supposed to be important . . . just weren't. At least not to me.

I thought it was fun to jump on the bed. If you jumped in just the right spot, it popped everyone on the bed high and then you'd tumble down onto the soft mattress. I loved the squeal of laughter that came out of my children's mouths.

We often took plastic shovels and buckets, hopped the creek, and traipsed through the fields to find treasure. Our treasure was old jelly glasses and cobalt blue medicine bottles buried at the back of the farm years earlier by someone else, but it was an adventure. I dug with my real shovel and they finished the job with their orange plastic shovels with the blue handles.

Summertime was when we explored, going to the library for special reading days, or swimming at the public pool. I remember clearly a mom chiding me because I dog-paddled in the middle of the pool while my toddlers jumped in. They had their floaties on and felt invincible. They weren't afraid of jumping into the deep, not as long as Mom was swimming there.

"Aren't you worried that they're jumping in like that? Don't you know how deep that water is?"

There were times that I thought I must be doing something wrong because I wasn't worrying enough.

"Aren't you worried that her teeth haven't come in yet?" (Like I could somehow schedule it.)

"Aren't you worried that if you let him play soccer only one season instead of two, he'll lose out on college scholarships one day?" (He was six.)

"Aren't you worried about your teenage daughter going on a mission trip in a foreign country?"

I grew up in a dysfunctional home. Later, my mom fought to be well, but growing up was chaotic and abusive and, often, scary. I sometimes hid my baby brother in the closet to keep him from hearing the fights or a belt whipping through the air.

When I became a mom to my first, I held the blond-haired, blue-eyed angel in my arms and prayed this prayer: "Thank you, God, for this miracle. Please help me to not mess this up."

So when other mothers asked me if I was worried, it made me wonder.

Should I be?

What I didn't realize then, and fully understand now, is that we are all different. Parenting truly is like a recipe from scratch. We bring what we have been given from our own parents, who we loved, and we discard what isn't useful. We read books. We go to classes. If we are lucky, we have other women who love us and who are there in a pinch with advice or encouragement.

Then you add in the uniqueness of each child, realizing that what works for one doesn't necessarily work for another. One child needs only a warning, while another needs a time-out or consequences.

And then there's us moms—the most unique ingredient of all. We have *some* experience. We have *some* natural giftings. Beyond the role of motherhood, we have those things that we love and bring to our children, like neatness or organization, adventure, a deep belief in Jesus, or in my case, a love for Jesus *and* jumping on the bed.

Put those together, add several years of hands-on parenting, and what comes out is a human being prepared for life on his or her own. Today I'm a grandma to five. The oldest is three, the youngest is eight months. For a while, it felt like it was raining grandbabies. It's the most fun part of who I am, being "Gaga."

If this wiser, older woman could go back to that young mom who once sat at the edge of the pool, who received the words, "Aren't you worried?" and made them her own, I'd tell her this: *They turned out well. I see a piece of you in each of them. One is an adventurer and tackles life with joy. Do you remember all those times you sat with your youngest daughter and read, and how she loved the flash cards while the others didn't? She's a professor now. And the child who you worried about most, because she was only nineteen months old when the twins were born? She's independent and giving, and you're going to love the woman she has become. Listen, Mom, it's hard work, and you aren't always going to have all the answers, but you don't have to be anybody but you. You will, with lots of prayer and trial and error, find what works the best for your family.*

I would have benefited from a book like this so many years ago. Kathy and Melinda are honest and encouraging, coming alongside as you love the children who are in your home right now, helping you mother from scratch.

—Suzanne (Suzie) Eller
speaker and author,
The Mom I Want to Be
www.tsuzanneeller.com

Acknowledgments

Thank you, God, for making Little League baseball boring enough for two moms to become lifelong friends.

We are so grateful to so many people who helped make this book possible.

To Mike, Molly, and Micah. To Ben, Max, Paul, Grace, and Luke. We couldn't have written this book without any of you. Thank you for being the catalysts for God's love and mercy in our lives. May you all know how much we treasure each and every one of you.

To the moms who graciously allowed us to share their thoughts and stories. Your transparency and wisdom are an inspiration to us and will be an encouragement to so many others.

Thank you to our agent, Blythe Daniel, for taking a chance on us and mentoring us. Your guidance and support through this process was priceless.

Thank you, Tim Peterson and Ellen Chalifoux, our editors at Bethany House, for caring about mothers and how they think.

Acknowledgments

Melinda
To my always interesting and entertaining husband, Mike, thank you for your unwavering support and belief in me. Love, Melinda

Kathy
Thank you, Ben, my soul mate, for always knowing that I had this in me. Your encouragement never ceases to amaze me. Love, Kathy

Introduction

How Did We Get Here?

We're not perfect mothers. We don't have perfect children. Who are we to claim we know anything about this mothering business? But who does Jesus use to minister to the masses? Wounded sinners, that's who. Now there's a label we can credibly embrace. God's Word tells us that Jesus chose to dine with the sinners and minister to the sick (Matthew 9:10; Mark 2:17). We know we would fit well at that table. We're hungry for women to receive God's grace in the area of mothering. When we willingly admit our flaws and insecurities, then we occupy that humble space where He can use us in spite of them.

We are passionate about sharing with other mothers the lessons we've learned and the grace God has shown us. On our blog, motheringfromscratch.com, we pursue our God-given mission to help mothers avoid what we have experienced over the years: isolation, guilt, and shame as we desperately try to do the best we can as moms. Our companion Facebook group, Moms Together (facebook.com/groups/momstogethergroup), also provides encouragement and hard-won wisdom on a variety of topics that are important to moms. We love the face-to-face contact we have with moms as we speak to MOPS and women's groups. These ministries led to *Mothering From Scratch*, the book.

Mothering From Scratch: Finding the Best Parenting Style for You and Your Family has been written, literally, on the kitchen tables of each other's homes. The same place where we feed our families is where we wanted to share with other moms the message that is in our hearts. After all, it was out of regular, everyday experiences—sharing our lives and families—that we found the mothering support and encouragement we needed.

Kathy

Back in 2007, as we watched our children play baseball, our friendship was born. I was a sorry mess. One strong wind and I was down like a house of cards. My trust in God was wavering; my confidence was at an all-time low. All I seemed to be able to do was make dinner and love on my children. Teenage boys, a preteen girl, and a sweet, active little four-year-old consumed me.

God knew I didn't want to befriend anyone, let alone someone who was taller and thinner than me. Yet He was working through Melinda all the while. I remember the reaction that I had in my mind when she told me she was writing for Christian publications. "How nice. How sweet," I said and sarcastically thought. It wasn't a compliment. I didn't understand how someone would devote her talents and passion to the Lord by writing—certainly not writing icky-sweet Christian women stuff. Eww. It's funny how this disgustingly nice person ended up talking me into going to a Christian writing conference and stoking a fire within my belly to write. After all, she had no belly to speak of, remember?

My heart had become rather hardened toward friendships with other women. They seemed difficult to get along with, and they always seemed to have it more together than I did. At first, I didn't think Melinda was any different, until I started talking to her. She was vulnerable, struggling like me, and very transparent with her feelings. It was quite refreshing. I could suddenly open up those dark places of mothering I didn't want to reveal. In doing so, the healing of my heart could begin. I could start enjoying motherhood again.

Melinda

I wasn't in much better shape than Kathy. I suffered from a general lack of confidence in my abilities. Why should mothering be any different? As my daughter hit the preteen years, I was also entering into a very exhausting and painful phase of parenting. Anything I thought I knew about mothering (which didn't seem like much) was quickly flying out the window.

My first vivid impression of Kathy was at the opening baseball practice. After someone agreed to fill in as coach of the team for a couple of weeks, she threw her hands up and yelled, "Thank you, Jesus!" Kathy's larger-than-life personality matched her red hair. Her loving but straightforward honesty and opinions were something I desperately needed in my mothering. And I didn't even know it.

I had a hard time feeling safe enough to share my mothering insecurities and mistakes with other women. I was ashamed and afraid of rejection. Somehow, Kathy made it safe to be brutally honest. I wasn't judged. Instead, I was loved and supported.

Two pale-faced women on those scorching-hot metal bleachers turned out to have way too much in common: We were both relatively intelligent, possessed an ironic and sometimes dark sense of humor, and found our salvation in Jesus Christ. I wasn't concerned about Kathy's conversion to Roman Catholicism. Kathy didn't question my poufy Beth Moore hair. We knew it was all about Jesus.

At each baseball practice we shared lively stories—okay, trials and tribulations—regarding mothering our kids. We found great comfort in discovering that neither of us was particularly confident or skilled at the task.

Our well-coiffed hair and shiny glossed lips served as an attractive camouflage for the insecurities that lay beneath. We were both ripe for an honest, transparent friendship—a dual mentorship where we could minister to each other's unaddressed weaknesses.

During one of our conversations, I shared that my mother had died of cancer a few years back. Suddenly, it was clear why I seemed to find mothering particularly perplexing. The absence of a mother—even as an adult—created a chronic, painful void that colored everything. And while Kathy's mother was a phone call away, distance prevented her daily presence and involvement in Kathy's life.

Gradually, we realized that we could each help fill the void in the other. We needed support to discover how to mother the way God designed us. Not the way we thought we should mother, or according to the latest parenting fad, but finding peace and confidence in our unique, God-given personalities and our children's.

Our own self-condemnation was a major barrier in this process. We both feared that maybe we had made such a mess of certain areas that we couldn't be redeemed. That somehow our mothering deficits had irreversibly damaged our children in some way. We still struggle with this thought pattern to some extent, but as we've obeyed God's direction in this new way of mothering, He has been faithful to show how He is merciful.

Our goal is that after you turn the last page, you'll be cooking out of your own cupboard, depending on God's power, guidance, and grace. Together, we'll show you how to understand yourself as a unique creation of God, find help through others, and work within your personality strengths. All the while, we promise to honor our commitment to stay in a place of transparency and humility.

Welcome to the Mothering Kitchen

Chapter 1
New Motherhood Starts With a New Plan

In many ways, the Gospel message can be applied to motherhood. We all fall short as moms—just like we do as God's children. Our salvation comes as we admit our need, realize we can't do it without Him, and resolve to change. And then we still screw up! Often. *Sigh.* Thankfully, God gives us new opportunities each day—each moment—to rewrite our mothering recipe. To add different, sometimes sweeter, ingredients and remove some of the bitter ones.

We can claim the truth of Lamentations 3:23 (NLT) that promises us, "Great is his faithfulness; his mercies begin afresh each morning."

Melinda

Once, long, long ago, I was Mommy-Know-It-All. Sure, back then in the heady days of my parental superiority, I had only one child who was all of three weeks old. But for that brief, shining moment in time, it was a smug, glorious place to live.

I was at a friend's baby shower—one of the first times I'd been out since my own daughter was born. Adorable outfits and sweet-smelling presents were passed around to unanimous admiration from the group. Suddenly, a book by Dr. Dobson landed in my hands—yes, THE James Dobson—PhD, Child Psychologist, Family Therapist, Founder of Focus on the Family.

I arrogantly flipped through the book, the fruit of years of education, experience, and research, and shrugged my shoulders and thought, *Eh. I won't need this.*

Although I may have lacked confidence in other areas, I was convinced that mothering was different. I had a plan. My mother was loving, but an untreated chronic mental illness made for instability and a lack of nurturing that I was determined not to repeat. I had my recipe: take the ingredients I didn't like when I was a child, and use the opposite ones. It was foolproof.

At first, I felt like the Julia Child of mothering. Molly was a ridiculously easy baby. She rarely cried, slept through the night within weeks, took naps like clockwork, and was enchantingly adorable. Then came toddlerhood. Seemingly overnight, my chubby-faced cherub lost her wings. As most toddlers do, she became pouty, finicky, and demanding. Around this time, my son, Micah, was born. He cried incessantly and seldom slept. In addition, he threw up constantly and failed to gain weight. His pediatrician assured me that I was just a "nervous mom." Still, I couldn't shake the feeling something was seriously wrong. One day, after Micah hadn't kept anything down for twenty-four hours, I decided to change pediatricians. I called Dr. Ben's office. Dr. Ben also happened to be Kathy's husband.

At the first appointment, I immediately felt like I had an ally. "I don't know what's wrong with Micah, but I'm not going to rest until I find out," he told me. After weeks of countless tests and blood draws, Dr. Ben discovered the source of Micah's problems. Late one night, in a dark, lonely hospital waiting room, he delivered the devastating news: "Micah's cystic fibrosis test was positive."

We were to check in to All Children's Hospital the next day. By the time we completed all the paperwork and headed for Micah's floor, it was almost nighttime. When you're dealing with grief, the darkness carries a heaviness that makes everything seem even more depressing.

Lovin' Spoonful

Are you struggling? You're not alone. Your situation may be unique to you, but your fears are common. Remember: Isolation and self-condemnation are tools of the enemy, not of our loving God.

As we walked to Micah's room, I noticed that each door had an animal sticker by the child's name. When we got to Micah's door, I spotted his sticker and immediately felt tears well up in my eyes. It was such an insignificant thing. *But not to me.* It was a familiar little yellow duck with feathers sticking up on his head. We had decorated Micah's room several months *after* he was born. By that time, Micah had a personality and a shock of white-blond hair that stuck straight up. I chose bedding with that exact duck because it reminded me of him. It's funny the things that God can use to speak to you. He instantly said to my heart, "I see Micah. I know him intimately. I am here."

God's presence eased the pain of my grief and fear. And I *was* relieved that the struggle for an answer was over. However, a new kind of struggle quickly began. I became overwhelmed by the unknown future of raising this precious special-needs child. In the midst of toddler tantrums and chronic illness, my confidence faltered badly. Further, I had strong people-pleasing tendencies that quickly infiltrated my mothering. If Micah didn't want peas, I made carrots. If Molly wanted a toy in the store, I bought it. Because if I could only make them happy, perhaps the enchantment would return—along with the belief in my mothering skills. It was an exhausting, futile exercise that never produced the elusive payoff I craved.

I had such high expectations for my mothering. I'm an intelligent person. I thought that I would instinctively know what to do in every situation. I would always be patient. I expected I'd enjoy every aspect of mothering. I *was* a loving, nurturing person. What was wrong with me?

My people-pleasing made for a lot of inner turmoil. It filled a need in me for temporary approval and absence of conflict, but it was failing badly as a parenting philosophy. When my kids weren't compliant, I was out of my comfort zone. I didn't want them to be unhappy with me, so I would appease them. I became angry and resentful with them because I had to continually confront uncomfortable situations. I was even angrier with myself for not being more assertive. I had such guilt when I gave in to them. I knew it wasn't the right thing to do.

But I didn't know how to change.

Mothering made me look bad to myself. I was a nice girl who did nice things. Who was this insecure maniac screaming at my kids? Certainly not the mother I envisioned I would be. I was such a disappointment to myself.

I was too ashamed to tell anyone how much I was struggling. Instead, I began to devour any Christian parenting book I could find. Books wouldn't judge me. Perhaps I could find the winning formula, implement it, and no one would be the wiser. Instead, my search led to mixed results, leaving me feeling overwhelmed, isolated, and like an even bigger failure.

The formulas weren't working. I had to come up with my own.

Here's the problem: I was scared. Terrified. Fear was getting in the way of my parenting.

Looking back, my new-mommy ignorance was bliss. If I had only known the breathtaking complexity of the challenges that lay ahead, I would have promptly added Dr. Dobson to speed dial and begged him to make house calls.

A Clean Slate

While we may not want to repeat our past, we often don't know how to break free from repeating unhealthy habits and patterns

Lovin' Spoonful

As moms, we can often feel we're never enough. Pray this prayer of grace:

> Lord, let me see myself the way You see me.
> Instill in my heart a holy view of who I am rather than one that makes me feel hopeless and inadequate.
> I am not perfect, but You are.
> Thank You for creating me just the way I am.
> Remind me to draw on Your grace and wisdom for both myself and my children. Amen.

from our history. Some of us are moms battling to "do it all right" after being wronged as young girls. Others of us have personalities totally different from our mothers. We can't quite figure out why we aren't as happy as our moms were while using their mothering recipe. Still others of us would say that our mothers did a lot well. However, we've found parenting starkly different from what we envisioned and are struggling to know how to mother effectively in this new reality. Further, we've found that motherhood is stretching and challenging our character in ways we weren't expecting.

Those internal and external mothering battles can lead to a steady stream of feelings of failure and inadequacy. What if we believe we've already made a mess of things? We all need to develop and find confidence in a new way of doing things—our own. But where do we begin? How will we know what's right for us and our families? No matter where we are in our mothering journey or what mistakes we believe we've made, we can all start mothering from scratch. A clean slate, so to speak. We can release ourselves from the pressure of following formulas and comparing ourselves to other moms. God will give us the wisdom and grace to mother the way He made us.

Developing a new plan requires courage, self-examination, trial and error, and the willingness to accept some helping hands along the way. When we invite the Holy Spirit to lead and empower us in this process, joy and faith in our mothering will naturally result. Ephesians 3:20 tells us that He "is able to do immeasurably more than all we ask or imagine."

It's not an easy thing, finding our own way in Christ, facing inadequate parts of ourselves, learning who we are as moms. But none of us are meant to do it alone. That's one of the things that got so many of us in trouble in the first place, right? Motherhood is a ministry. And Jesus never sent out His children to minister alone. But where do we find supportive fellow travelers? Do they exist? For many years, we didn't think so.

In past generations, moms found support and wisdom in their mothers and grandmothers, who were close by and available. More recently, moms were able to find an older woman willing to invest regular time in guiding them. But today's reality is that families are scattered and often broken. The pace of our lives doesn't allow for the structure and time investment of days gone by. The time has come for a new kind of encouragement and instruction (often called mentoring). We need an approach that better fits our current mothering reality.

> No matter where we are in our mothering journey or what mistakes we believe we've made, we can all start mothering from scratch.

Finding quality instruction from trustworthy people who share the same values can seem impossible. We have to get out of our own way, moms. Let's quit the habit of constantly comparing our successes and failures to other moms'. It either gives us a false sense of pride or makes us feel horribly inadequate. Who needs that? It doesn't serve us, or our children, well. Through God's grace, we have to let down those barriers that hold us back from being vulnerable and teachable. As we ask His guidance in this process, our eyes will be opened to people and circumstances from which we can gain support, tools, and knowledge. And we'll find support in a variety of settings and from a group of people we never thought we could learn from or influence.

From Confident to Clueless

Kathy

Let me share my story. The year was 1983. I was thirteen, MTV was two years old, and Michael Jackson moonwalked to "Billie Jean" for the first time. My eighteen-year-old sister was pregnant. It was enough to cure me from ever wanting to have a baby before getting married. Despite my ego-driven embarrassment, I received an amazing gift: my niece, little Lindsey-Ann.

> Motherhood is a ministry. And Jesus never sent out His children to minister alone.

Her nose was the size of my pinky nail. She had sweet, cocoa-colored eyes and a cute flip of brown hair. I had no real responsibility, just the butterflies in my tummy and a new, warm feeling when she slept on my chest.

She grew up in my selfish, adolescent little world. There, I learned how to care for her. She was my sister-baby: not really my little sister, but sister-like nonetheless. I felt pain in my heart when I would hear her cry in the middle of the night. Sometimes I would get up and warm her bottle. One night, as I rushed to soothe her, I accidentally warmed it too much, scalding her mouth. I cried and cried as I held her in the dark. I didn't tell anyone; they might not trust me to care for her again. She's in her thirties now. I'm still apologizing to her for burning her little mouth.

We (my mother, my sister, and my stepfather) cared for Lindsey for the first few years of her life in our home. It was then that I received the most important training for how to mother. Side by side, my mother and older sister showed me how to diaper, feed, rock, and love a baby. "The most important job in the world is taking care of children," my mother always said. "Don't you forget it."

My "most important job" started in 1993. My husband was a first-year pediatric resident in South Carolina. Max Benjamin was about to arrive, and I was *ready*—like a plump Thanksgiving turkey.

What more did I need to know? I had practically raised my niece during her first years of life. My devoted husband was a pediatric resident physician. I had cared for numerous children over the years. *I needed to start my job. I needed to be important.*

I thought I had it all figured out. Sure, I was important, but I quickly found that I was completely clueless regarding the difficulty and intensity of this mothering business now that *I* was the mom.

The new reality of nights of endless feedings, self-imposed isolation, and piles of breeding laundry left me wondering how I was going to do this. Max was a chunky, luscious baby boy who was growing before my eyes. But I was growing in discontentment—and felt enormous guilt. When Max was ten months old, we decided we didn't want him to be alone much longer. He needed a playmate. Nineteen months after Max was born, we welcomed our son Paul to the family. These boys were an enormous blessing. But I still couldn't shake my feelings of being discontent and overwhelmed. This wasn't about them. This was about me. These kinds of demands had never been placed on me. I had set myself up for failure by believing I could do everything by myself. After all, this was what I felt like I was born to do! So why did I feel like I was going crazy?

 Lovin' Spoonful

Feeling overwhelmed by all the images and statuses online that present picture-perfect homes and families? It's time for a change in perspective. Walk away from the computer. Instead, open your Bible. Pray. You'll be amazed at your change in mind-set.

Why wasn't this working for me? My pre-mommy confidence was long gone. It was replaced by merely surviving. My babies were happy. My pediatrician husband was ecstatic. Somehow, I had to find a way to mother that encouraged me to feel the same way.

Who's to Blame?

We love our children. We want to be good mothers. But sheer desire is not enough. It's not our fault if we lack certain knowledge and skills in the mothering arena. Maybe we feel guilty we're not fully satisfied with our roles as moms.

Perhaps we have the knowledge and skills but are overwhelmed by the magnitude of mothering. We find ourselves simply surviving day after day instead of deliberately engaging in a sacred vocation. Or maybe we think, considering the training we've had, we're doing as good as can be expected. We're getting by. Still, we have that nagging feeling that it could or should be better.

> God wants to show us a better way. All aspects of mothering are skills that can be acquired by anyone willing to learn.

What do we do with that feeling? Resign ourselves to it? Find ways to escape? Stay negative and resentful? God wants to show us a better way. All aspects of mothering are skills that can be acquired by anyone willing to learn. When we rely on God's power, He'll show and equip us to discover a satisfying way to care for His children that's unique to each of us.

We were going to be a living Johnson's baby commercial! And then I had my baby. You don't realize how much you don't know until you're on your journey. And then a new day comes with something else you don't know. I try to remember the saying "There is no way to be a perfect mother but a million ways to be a good one."

—Heather, mother of two

31

Notes:

- You probably noticed the "Lovin' Spoonfuls" throughout this chapter. These are little bites of encouragement and wisdom—short takeaways you can apply to your mothering immediately. You'll find more throughout the book.

- At the end of each chapter is a "Stirring Your Thoughts" section. This has questions for you to reflect on personally or discuss with a group.

- "Let's Get Cookin'" are action steps that help you think through and put into practice the principles and concepts we discuss in each chapter.

- All names used throughout the book have been changed, unless otherwise noted.

Stirring Your Thoughts

1. When have you been overconfident in your mothering? What happened as a result?

2. What are some things you've done as a mom simply because it was all you knew?

3. Briefly describe the mothering recipe that was handed down to you.

4. In what ways would you like your mothering experience to be different?

5. Do you feel you've had mothering mentors? If so, who? If not, think of two mothers from whom you can learn.

6. Where have you lacked key instruction in mothering?

7. Are you open to instruction in your mothering? Is your heart teachable? Why or why not?

Let's Get Cookin'

When our hearts are teachable, we can avoid unnecessary pain. We also benefit from the fellowship and insights of others around us. Here are some action steps to move toward opening and/or healing our hearts:

- On a daily (even moment-to-moment) basis, ask the Holy Spirit to keep your heart open. Ask Him to open your eyes and tune your ears to His guidance as you interact with others.

- If your heart is wounded, you can gain the courage to risk rejection and failures with God's help. We highly recommend reading Suzanne Eller's *The Unburdened Heart* and *The Mended Heart*. These are two of the best books we know on forgiveness and healing.

- If you're depressed, seek clinical help immediately. If you're exhausted or overwhelmed, reach out to others for support. Keep reading. We'll give you practical, doable ways to find help and connection in chapter 9.

Chapter 2

All Mothers Can Start
From Scratch

Perhaps we feel we need improvement in a few areas of our mothering. Maybe we believe we're completely failing in others. There is good news! No matter where we are in our mothering journey, a new era of motherhood can start today. What a relief, right? *It's not too late*. All mothers can start from scratch—regardless of the age of our children.

It doesn't matter how many times we've fought the same battles or made the same mistakes, it *can* be different. Isaiah 43:19 gives us great assurance of God's willingness to empower us on this journey: "See, I am doing a new thing! Now it springs up; do you not perceive it? I am making a way in the wilderness and streams in the wasteland."

Each moment provides new opportunities to make different, grace-filled, God-driven choices. It may be hard. It may, at times, require more courage and endurance than we think we've got. But we don't have to do it alone. So exactly where and how do we begin?

How Does God Transform Gut-Busting Guilt Into Grace?

It all starts with a teachable heart—one that's open and willing to embark on the lifelong process of surrender to God's leading and direction. This heart of surrender doesn't form overnight; it begins with a conscious choice. It might be as simple as saying, "God, please help me. I need you." Be warned. This requires us to put on our big-girl pants. God-driven choices aren't necessarily comfortable or convenient. They often require sacrifice and courage. However, God's response to our obedience will not disappoint.

Melinda

My first step toward surrender began years ago, in the middle of the night. Exhausted and overcommitted, I heard God's still, small voice say to my heart, "What are you doing?" It was gentle, not accusatory. And it broke my stubborn resolve to do things my way. I responded with something like, "I'm running myself into the ground. And I'm ready to change. Just tell me what to do."

Kathy

For me, I became constantly distracted. Any issue with my kids or life circumstance derailed me from being effective. I struggled with forming any kind of logical prayer. I found that God even listens and responds to my desperate, sometimes simple one-word prayers: *Help. Please. Thank you. Why?* My only goal was to ask. That's all I could do, especially during times of distraction.

A surrendered heart silences the voice of condemnation in our minds—the voice that tells us it's all up to us. That voice scares us to death! It tells us we're falling short. It's the one that says things will never get better. The one that convinces us we'll never measure up, that there's something inherently wrong with our character and it can't be fixed. The result can be hopelessness and paralysis. It makes us think to ourselves, *What's the use?*

Instead, we need to learn to recognize the voice of true *conviction*. It doesn't bellow like our two-year-old who wants attention.

Lovin' Spoonful

Remember how Jesus treated repentant women. When the crowd wanted to stone the adulterous woman, He stopped them in their tracks. "Jesus straightened up and asked her, 'Woman, where are they? Has no one condemned you?' 'No one, sir,' she said. 'Then neither do I condemn you,' Jesus declared. 'Go now and leave your life of sin'" (John 8:10-11). He offered grace and the hope that her life could be different.

Here's a simple guide to knowing if our guilt is from the Holy Spirit: Condemnation paralyzes; conviction energizes.

It's more like a gentle nudge, an eye-opening moment that inspires us to want to do things differently. Since it comes from God, we sense His assurance that we don't have to do it alone. Yes, maybe we've made mistakes, but we're not without hope. We become energized instead of paralyzed as a result.

Romans 8:1–2 assures us that our freedom has already been purchased. We just have to claim it. "Therefore, there is now no condemnation for those who are in Christ Jesus, because through Christ Jesus the law of the Spirit who gives life has set you free from the law of sin and death."

How Do We Slice and Dice Mommy Guilt?

Let's cut to the chase: Mommy guilt is a liar. It tells us that if only we had made all the right choices and done everything perfectly, we would've been able to produce all the right outcomes. It tells us that if we'll only try harder, the internal struggle will stop. Unfortunately, it's a false, misleading trap. No matter how hard we're trying, mommy guilt pushes us into thinking we could and should be trying harder. It pelts us with accusing thoughts like *Why can't*

I do this better? Why are everyone's kids more well-behaved than mine? What am I doing wrong? What am I missing? If I would've just started earlier, my kids wouldn't be making these choices.

Mommy guilt stems from an illusion that we're ultimately in control. Yes, we can guide and influence our children. But from the time they're very small, they're making their own choices. The way they process information, their perceptions of us, and their interpretation of the world around them are uniquely their own. No, we're not the boss of them all the time, especially in their little heads.

> A surrendered heart silences the voice of condemnation in our minds— the voice that tells us it's all up to us.

Melinda

For years, I lived under a cloud of mommy condemnation. I never felt like I was enough. At the same time, I had this misguided notion that all outcomes, good or bad, were the direct result of my actions. My humility is inspiring, right? If only I could do more for my children, be more for them, get it all right, they'd be perpetually happy and compliant. I believed that *their* displeasure at any given moment could somehow be traced back to *my* failure. I provided too much indulgence, too many second chances, and not enough responsibility. And yet their demands and discontent intensified.

 Lovin' Spoonful

Are you relying on the church or school to do the instruction that is your parental responsibility? Are you practicing what you preach or only giving lip service to your faith? Kids can spot a fake a mile away. Get real about your faith and share your struggles. That forms their view of God's love more than anything.

Ironically, I didn't see these behaviors as unhealthy or enabling. I was just trying to be a good mom and apparently failing badly. I always believed that it wasn't my approach that was badly flawed. It was me.

The "aha!" moment, the one that put me on the path to change and acceptance of God's grace, began with a question. Several years ago, my sister was visiting from out of town. After a couple of days, she looked at me and said simply, "Why are you still pouring Micah's cereal?" It was as if I'd been struck by lightning. Yes, why *was* I pouring my very capable, able-bodied, nearly pre-teen boy's cereal? Somehow that question opened my eyes to a host of other ways I was enabling my kids. Did I truly want to do what was best for my kids? Well, it *wasn't* pouring their cereal until they were in college. In that moment, it was as if Jesus simply said to my heart, "I was waiting for you to realize this, child."

No condemnation. No "What took you so long?" Just an invitation to walk a different path. Five years later, I'm still on that journey, propelled each day by His gentle conviction to make adjustments and always covered by His boundless grace.

Sometimes we don't even know where we need to change, we just wish we had some do-overs in certain areas. Maybe we just feel like we need a fresh perspective or approach. This calls for a loving process of self-examination. We'll be addressing various aspects of this process, one by one, throughout this book.

After we go to God with our shortcomings and He convicts us of those areas where we need to ask for forgiveness, let's look at what we should do next. Our moral obligation is to take action regarding whatever we did to wrong our kids. Perhaps they're not old enough to confess to and seek forgiveness from, but we can still stay accountable to God through the rest of the reconciliation process. There's great danger in taking a passive approach of enabling or overcompensating for the offense or shortcoming, wishing it hadn't happened or believing that our kids will simply forget it. Being in a state of denial is no way to mother a child.

Our God and Savior died for us so we can move away from sin and repent, not sweep it under a spiritual rug and hope it doesn't affect anyone ever again.

Other times, we take responsibility for more than we should. You name it, a mom will feel guilt about it. From how we diaper and feed our kids to our choices regarding working outside the home. Our female, human hearts are quick to turn our past "transgression" into today's scapegoat. When we face a difficult behavior or phase with our children, we search for how we could've prevented it. We try to trace it back and pinpoint what we could've done differently. We often conclude that we're somehow to blame. We think we deserve this turmoil we're going through. We take responsibility for their struggles and make excuses for them. After all, they wouldn't be acting like this if we hadn't been so impatient, distracted, demanding, etc., would they? Internal punishment replaces heartfelt, God-driven change.

You name it, a mom will feel guilt about it.

That's not how God works. That's why Jesus came. Whatever we did wrong with our children in the past, we have to do what's right for them *now*. While it may temporarily relieve our guilt, our unwillingness to set boundaries and hold them accountable for their behaviors doesn't do them any favors. It's pretty selfish actually. We should know. We did it for years.

Breaking Free From Condemnation

We can't control what has happened in the past. Yet we try to console ourselves into thinking that "this" will make up for "that." Doesn't that ignore that He has cast our sins "as far as the east is from the west" (Psalm 103:12)? Jesus died for freedom from mommy guilt, too. He cares about our tender souls as much as the criminals beside Him on Calvary.

Kathy

I have some beautiful memories of early motherhood, but some of them aren't so inspiring. I've lived with the guilt that the bad times outweighed the good times more often than not. I experienced traumatic postpartum depression after the births of my children. It haunted me as a mother. Could I have prevented it? Why didn't I get treatment earlier? What damage did I do to my children because I was untreated and muddling through motherhood?

Here's what I've learned: Some of those questions will never be answered. When we're struggling as moms, that's when God takes over, sometimes through changing our circumstances, sometimes through other people.

Many of my early memories of my children's lives are cloudy because of depression. I often pray that God would reveal those memories to me as consolation for what I may have missed or misunderstood. My unwell, clouded mind told me that depression was my fault. It told me that I should be able to "get myself together," or it said I would never get better, so I should just get used to feeling lousy about everything, including being a mom. Those feelings of condemnation led to emotional and physical isolation, refusing to ask for real help (at least not for more than a frozen lasagna), and wallowing in overall self-pity.

When I finally sought active treatment through therapy and medication, the grip that depression had over my mothering loosened. God granted me the conviction that He entrusted these children to me. I had to get well. I couldn't stay in some dark place in my mind because I was ashamed of how I felt about mothering. There was no overnight healing. No eureka moment. God placed people in my life, mostly my dear husband, who challenged me to treat the real problem: the depression. My children have shared some of their memories of me during those times. Some are painful; some are liberating. I've tried to make peace with knowing I can only deal with any aftereffects as they occur, as they surface, and that God will give me the strength and wisdom to do so.

We can't go back and change history. The "if onlys" and "I should haves" aren't productive change agents. With God's help, we can break out of our paralysis and take concrete steps to act on our convictions now. *Here's how:*

Ask yourself about regret. Here's a strategy: Ask yourself, "What do I need to do *now* in order to look back on this time with no regrets?" You don't want to look back ten years from now, or even one day from now, and want a redo. When we're struggling and overwhelmed, this helps us focus on what's really important.

Melinda

One of my biggest regrets is not spending more time just playing with and nurturing my kids when they were younger. I was so stressed, impatient, and self-condemning. I was driven by people pleasing and obligation. I regret not being more "in the moment" when they were small. Ever since I realized this, I've been trying to be more present with my children.

Seek support. Neither of us did nearly enough of this, especially as moms of young children, when we were so susceptible to isolation and feelings of insecurity.

Kathy

The early years of being a mom were difficult for me. Now (my kids are twenty-one, nineteen, fifteen, and eleven) I realize that my regret is not the time and energy I put into mothering, but rather the lack of support that I sought out for myself. I should've solicited help in areas of life that were difficult for me so I could better focus. I should've stayed closer to God. I didn't know how. No one told me I could have assistance without feeling handicapped. No one showed me how to maintain my spirituality in the midst of chaos.

Start with one. This helps when we're overwhelmed by too many areas we want to change at once. For example, maybe we want to undo some enabling behaviors with our children. We can start by asking them to pack their own lunches. Or we can have them match socks while they're watching TV. The idea is to start somewhere, no matter how small.

Where's the Sweetness in Imperfection?

If we were perfect mothers, we'd be insufferable. We'd lack compassion and be fooled into thinking we have no need for God or each other.

Our children need to observe a mother who regularly accepts God's grace and forgiveness and offers them the same. Romans 8:28 promises us, "In all things God works for the good of those who love him, who have been called according to his purpose." The mistakes we've made, the ways we feel we've fallen short, are part of our children's journeys and can be redeemed by their heavenly Father. We're going to fail them. Guaranteed. That's why we have to keep pointing them toward Jesus, who never will.

Here's another sweet point: Imperfection breeds humility. Our kids will understand that God's grace is easily accessible. We can model the idea of asking for forgiveness and show firsthand the power of the Holy Spirit and His ability to change us—in an up close and personal way. That directly impacts their everyday lives.

 Lovin' Spoonful

Were you a rebellious teenager? Have you struggled with drug and alcohol abuse? Does your past include sexual sin you're ashamed of? If God wants you to share these struggles with your children, He'll lead you to do so. Either way, move forward assured of His grace and mercy and He'll strengthen you.

It impacts their view of God. It mirrors a fraction of God's forgiveness of us.

Marie, a single mom of two young boys, held guilt for a long time about failing in her ability to teach her sons how to be men. "Eventually, God showed me that I'm not their dad. I'm their mom, so I can only be the best mom I can be. I quit trying to be what I could not."

But here's another sweet reward about regret: We get to share it with others so they don't make the same mistakes. That's the sweetness in our failings. Marie agrees: "Looking back, my decision to get married was fueled by all the wrong reasons. But it gave my sons and me a wealth of experience that God is using and will continue to use to help me and others avoid future mistakes. I love it when I have the opportunity to counsel others in areas I've fallen short."

> If we were perfect mothers, we'd be insufferable.

God's capacity to redeem our mistakes is infinite. Joel 2:25 assures us, "I will repay you for the years the locusts have eaten."

I also firmly believe that we can start anew at any given moment—we just have to make that choice. There is no rule book when it comes to mothering, and every child is so different that what works for one won't necessarily work for the other.

—Tammy, mother of two

Stirring Your Thoughts

1. If you could have a conversation with yourself pre-kids, what would you tell yourself to do differently?
2. What are three areas where you feel you're currently falling short?
3. What are some nuggets of wisdom that you can share with other moms in this stage of mothering?

4. Ask yourself why you're currently making the choices you're making now (schooling options, discipline techniques, work schedule, routines, etc.). Which ones are within your control? Which ones aren't?

5. What's one area where you haven't set clear boundaries that consistently affects your family?

6. Do you parent in survival mode? Is this a new pattern for you, or is it an old problem surfacing in new situations?

7. Are you setting a consistent example for your children? Do your actions match your words?

Let's Get Cookin'

• Pick one of the three areas you identified for improvement or that you feel convicted to change. Brainstorm three small, tangible changes you can implement this week.

• What more could you ask for than the wisdom of another mom sharing what she wishes she would've done differently? We encourage you to ask questions 1, 2, and 3 from "Stirring Your Thoughts" to other moms. (And please share what you learn with us!)

• In our second "Stirring Your Thoughts" step, we asked you to identify three areas where you're falling short. If it's age appropriate and you feel led by God, ask your children for their forgiveness in these areas. Explain to them how you plan to change.

Chapter 3
What Happens When You Feel Like You're Not a Good Mom?

Our minds are often a battlefield between feeling and fact. As moms, our internal dialogue can be overwhelming at times, telling us how we've fallen short, the things we should or shouldn't have done, reminding us of all the moms who seem to do it better. It goes on and on. As impossible as it seems, we *can* gain control of our minds. Motherhood is an incredible opportunity for us to draw closer to God. We can either choose to allow our feelings to condemn us or we can allow them to propel us to continual dependence on God's power and grace.

The reality of our inadequacies can smack us in the face. Children don't try to be reflections of our character. They're just natural little mirrors. They show us both the pretty and smart parts of us and the unattractive, hidden ones. Becoming mothers gives us a unique opportunity to make a gigantic leap in our moral development. Goals such as worldly success and recognition become less important. We're not suggesting that this happens quickly or automatically. It requires a change in our mind-set. During these years of mothering, our lives become less about us and more about following the mandate to love, nurture, and discipline our children through the power of the Holy Spirit. Moving closer to God helps us recognize the greater goal of raising children who can make a difference—and perhaps further new, healthier legacies than what we were given. Now is the time to lean heavily on God for His direction and desires for us as women and moms.

Melinda

Mom self-talk can be brutal. When my son was in second grade, his school was putting on a Christmas performance. We arrived, greeted by a sea of boys dressed in white shirts. Micah was wearing *plaid*. In all the holiday hoopla, I had misread the memo from Micah's teacher as "have your child wear a dress shirt" instead of "have your child wear a *white* dress shirt."

> Children don't try to be reflections of our character. They're just natural little mirrors.

In my mind, Micah might as well have been wearing a T-shirt emblazoned with "I'm dressed like this because my mother is a moron." He looked like he wanted to be swallowed up into a black hole. I would've gladly joined him. Finally, I came to my senses. My mom problem-solving skills kicked into turbo drive. I jumped in the car and headed to Kmart.

On the drive over, Satan began to have a field day in my head. *Why do I do things like this? Every other mother managed to figure out how to dress her child. Why am I such an idiot?*

I found the shirt and ran to the checkout line, where the clerk asked me, "Is there some kind of program at one of the local schools? You have no idea how many moms have been in here in the last hour buying white shirts!"

We'll have these experiences our entire mothering lives. Mothering requires a level of self-denial, but it also requires a continuous

Lovin' Spoonful

Lie: My fidgety child will never learn to sit still.

Truth: He may be fidgety today, but someday his focus will improve.

Lie: My teenager who listens to music I don't like will never learn to appreciate things of true value.

Truth: Like all of us, she is a work in progress.

Lie: My child will never embrace his faith.

Truth: God has a hold on his heart that I can't see.

Lie: I will always lose my temper with my children.

Truth: I can't change overnight, but one moment at a time, I can make better choices.

process of receiving His grace. This is a learned behavior that requires constant petitions to the Holy Spirit. We need His power to enable us to view ourselves the way God sees us. When we've lost our temper with our kids or simply feel like we are not measuring up to the mom we think we should be, we are incredibly vulnerable to the enemy's condemnation.

We have to put the accuser in his place. In *Duty or Delight? Knowing Where You Stand with God*, author Tammie Head challenges us to refute the voices in our head by saying this: "You know what? That is not my God. The way I'm feeling is not my God. That's not God's voice in my heart. That's not the way my God thinks toward me. That is not what my God would say to me. My God doesn't feel that way about me."[1] It's also helpful to memorize Scripture. Refuting the lie is great; however, replacing it with truth is what truly sets us free.

No other life transition compares to suddenly being responsible for another little helpless person's needs. We simply can't do it without calling on God's strength and the support of others.

How Can We Adjust Our Expectations?

The mothering legacy passed down to us may have left us with more butterflies in our stomachs than confidence in our skills. What if the expertise we possess in the workplace or other arenas dwarfs the level of competency we feel as mothers? When it comes to mothering, we tend to blame ourselves when things don't measure up to our expectations. We compare ourselves to other moms and our children to their children and wonder what we're doing wrong. Others' expectations of us can also sometimes feel suffocating. Are we missing something? Does this mean we're horrible moms?

We tend to judge our success halfway through the hands-on period of mothering, rather than when it's finished. If our ten-year-old can't organize her backpack, it doesn't mean that she won't ever be able to hold down a job. Always bear in mind that our children aren't finished products. They're unique individuals who aren't all suited for the same activities—or for the pursuits that *we* enjoy. This is an opportunity to refute the unrealistic expectations and the condemnation that often accompanies them and "take captive every thought to make it obedient to Christ" (2 Corinthians 10:5).

For example, during the 1990s (yes, that means we're quite seasoned), the parenting trends in Christian circles were centered around rigid discipline strategies, techniques, and schedules. We knew our children's personalities and were reluctant to implement these approaches. Just as we suspected, they did not suit our personalities or our children's. Yet when these strategies didn't work, we still blamed ourselves. We felt like mommy failures who had surely doomed our children to selfishness, rebellion, and the inability to think creatively.

We don't have bad kids. We aren't bad moms. We just sometimes need to adjust our formulas. We've both discovered we often have to give up our ideas of the way we think things should be or what others are telling us to do in order to embrace the reality of our personalities and our children's temperaments. This is a necessary and grace-filled approach. As moms, we can become skilled at making accommodations. Ask for the Holy Spirit's guidance and follow the instincts He gives you, even if it doesn't conform to your ideal or others' expectations.

How Do Children Change Our Character?

Having children requires a change in mind-set from *me* to *we*. Some would like to tell you that this is a negative force in your life, squeezing out some sense of identity from you. There is loss and gain associated with every major life change/experience. Motherhood brings the addition of a new person. Indeed, that new person includes *you*. Rather than a barrier to our personal development, children can be the very vessels God uses to shape our characters to bring us closer to Him. It's not a positive/negative—it's a shift in responsibility, and a great one at that.

> Always bear in mind that our children aren't finished products.

Mothers don't voluntarily sign up for a character change. God seems to make it happen ever so effectively through mothering children. Are you impatient? Here's a difficult child. Are you insecure about your worth? An independent kid is just the ticket. Are you struggling with selfishness? A demanding, needy child can cure that. Somehow, the magnitude of raising children gets us moving in a more godly direction and away from focusing on our own desires and strength.

Meet Laura. She is an achiever. One of her top strengths is her ability to get things done. "It makes me a great person to have on a team at work or as a teacher," the mother of four says. "But motherhood isn't something you achieve. We never 'arrive' as moms. There's no sense of finishing it. So how do I use my strength in a job that ignores it and makes it feel irrelevant?"

She has found this struggle especially difficult as she raises two girls with trauma and neglect issues from their early years in foster care. "One of the girls has required intense intervention and

Lovin' Spoonful

The demands of motherhood can cause us to view our children as barriers to our goals, personal development, and productivity. Say a simple prayer to transform your attitude:

> Dear God, allow my heart to recognize my children as divinely given molders of my character. Let me see Your Holy Spirit working through them to change me. Amen.

therapeutic parenting for the past eight years—and we're maybe three inches further down the road with her anxiety and behavior challenges," Laura says. "I often have conversations with God about why He purposefully built me a certain way and has rewarded it in so many other arenas. But then, in the longest-lasting, most personally challenging role of my life, He seems to make it a liability. I think part of it may be so I don't try to do things on my own apart from Him. It's also helped me to stake my intrinsic value on Whose I am, rather than what I do. This is still a daily struggle for me."

Our prayer can be to become more Christ-shaped and less "me-shaped." The new woman you become is still *you*, only better. God is choosing this life, this family, this time for His purpose through you. If we look through the eyes of our kids, we should always be the best version of ourselves. Being a patient person is more important than having well-behaved children. Finding our worth in Christ is more valuable than feeling good about our achievements. Serving our families helps get the "me" out of the way to do God's work.

How Do We Make Peace With the Uncomfortable?

God makes many promises. Effortless motherhood is not one of them. Mothers who go into parenting with the notion that they can set their children on autopilot, or conversely, that they can control every detail of their kids' physical, emotional, and spiritual beings are in for an interesting and exhausting ride. We need more cheerleaders and support to help us confront the uncomfortable parts of mothering. People who call us out help us identify and hold us accountable on the issues that are negatively affecting our families.

Melinda

When my daughter turned five, I had a princess birthday party for her. I even made silver hats with tulle "plumes" floating out the top. I planned elaborate regal details of every kind. This was when I was still trying to regain the enchantment in my mothering. A good friend of mine came with her young daughter. Throughout the party, she was extremely helpful—even anticipating needs and potential problems before they occurred. Yet somehow this made me feel "less than" or like I didn't have it all together (which I didn't, but I was also still in my denial phase). Later, we talked about it. She apologized (which wasn't really necessary) and shared that she struggled with control issues that weren't good for her family or the other relationships in her life. She asked me to keep her accountable when I noticed this behavior in her. Conversely, she held me accountable with my people-pleasing weakness, as well as my tendency to blame myself for every mothering mishap.

This is what real support looks like. It requires honesty, humility, and accountability. It's tempting to excuse or rationalize our weaknesses and not share them with anyone. Many of us have said in overwhelmed weariness, "I can't worry about that today," or, "I'm going to let that behavior go this one time." Maybe your personality hates conflict. We see an issue that needs to be confronted and tell ourselves that we'll have more courage to tackle it another day. Or we may spend too much time simply moving from crisis to crisis. We've both been mothers long enough to see the fruit of ignoring these unhealthy thinking patterns in ourselves and in our children.

Our role is to be facilitators for who God has designed our children to be—not for *our* purposes or fulfillment, but for His.

Lovin' Spoonful

Overcompensation as defined by Merriam-Webster: excessive compensation; *specifically*: excessive reaction to a feeling of inferiority, guilt, or inadequacy leading to an exaggerated attempt to overcome the feeling.[2]

We can't do this if we're not confronting our own struggles and are trying to shape our children into our own vision. So how do we respond when our children have incredibly different goals, personalities, and/or gifts from ours? The answer is constant recalibration and seeking humility and guidance from their Creator. We can also seek assistance from others who can help foster those gifts and character traits that may be foreign to us. It often requires us to break out of our personal comfort zones.

Kathy

For example, I don't have an athletic bone in my body. And I shudder performing music publicly. However, all of my kids are athletes and musicians. It was a difficult transition for me. I was forced to move from protective mommy to cheering spectator and from an anxious musician to enjoying the performance. My husband gave me strict instructions: Keep my butt on the bleachers unless 9-1-1 is called, and pace in the back of the room instead of sweating bullets in the front row. Just because I was squirrely in these arenas didn't mean I should pass that insecurity on to my kids.

Melinda

My daughter's personality is very different from mine in a number of areas. She has a huge need for social interaction. While I love being around people, I also enjoy solitude. I always have, even as a teenager. Molly has no need for solitude. Socializing is a priority.

Although I had to put some boundaries on this need—and I, personally, look on in exhaustion—I learned to appreciate and understand how important it was to her happiness and expression of herself.

Our personalities, and the personalities of our children, are uniquely and beautifully God-made. When we learn to filter out truth from lies and adjust our expectations, it sets everyone free. We're able to be who God created us to be instead of trying to squeeze ourselves into molds that only make us feel inadequate and condemned. When we center our minds on truth and choose to be obedient to God, He will use our children to mold us as much as we hope that we're shaping His children.

> Our role is to be facilitators for who God has designed our children to be—not for **our** purposes or fulfillment, but for His.

I am totally different in so many ways now that I'm a mom. One of the biggest [changes] for me is how less selfish I am now. I used to pray for more patience, and then I was given a special-needs child—instant, life-changing patience was achieved.

—Taylor, mother of three

Stirring Your Thoughts

1. What did you dream motherhood would be like?
2. In what ways did you have difficulty tapping in to your motherly instincts?
3. Have you ever felt like you just weren't cut out for this? How?
4. How can you combat those "bad mom" thoughts that try to condemn and discourage you?
5. How has motherhood changed your character?
6. How can you seek God's wisdom in passing down a healthy legacy?

Let's Get Cookin'

An Accountability Checklist

- In which of the following areas could you use some accountability?

  ___ Controlling tendencies

  ___ People pleasing

  ___ Overprotection

  ___ Perfectionism

  ___ Enabling

  ___ Other _____

- Think and pray about someone whom you could ask to keep you accountable in one or more of these areas. Write down their name(s) and call them. Don't just put it in your planner or in your phone as a "to-do" item. Act on it right now. Nope, don't just email. Call them so you have the one-on-one time on the phone.

- Schedule weekly or monthly check-ins with this person or persons. Just knowing that you're being held accountable can often improve your attitude and your actions.

Section
II

The Spicy Realities
of Motherhood

Chapter 4
Mothering the Way You're Made

God's design is perfect. He created us. Does it make us perfect? In a sense, yes. We're who He uniquely chose to mother our children. We can't improve on God's design. Yet often we try to squeeze ourselves into molds of motherhood that don't fit. The result is frustration and anxiety. However, when we embrace who God made us, we find a great level of joy and security and a deeper relationship with our Creator.

Kathy

When I'm around people, I'm energized. I'm also creative and very organizationally challenged (a fancy way of saying scattered and messy). These strong personality traits didn't mesh well with being a stay-at-home, always-in-the-house mom. I didn't enjoy being isolated. Who would? When I felt overwhelmed by the day-to-day tasks that needed to be done, home seemed very claustrophobic. My need for lots of interaction with others was difficult to meet when I had little ones who needed a predictable, peaceful home life.

Lovin' Spoonful

In his grace, God has given us different gifts for doing certain things well. So if God has given you the ability to prophesy, speak out with as much faith as God has given you. If your gift is serving others, serve them well. If you are a teacher, teach well. If your gift is to encourage others, be encouraging. If it is giving, give generously. If God has given you leadership ability, take the responsibility seriously. And if you have a gift for showing kindness to others, do it gladly.

Romans 12:6–8 (NLT)

To help alleviate my guilt and angst, I decided to try other things outside of my role as Mom. You name it, I tried it. Private tutoring, working full time as Ben's office manager, teaching classes through my local Catholic diocese. I even opened a home decorating business because I thought I was passionate enough about it. No matter what I tried, the mama grass never became greener. I constantly searched for a shiny new penny anywhere in my life to distract me. What I really needed was to stop searching for ways to avoid motherhood. After all, I loved my kids! Slowly, I developed a different, more "Kathy" way of doing things. It took me years to finally embrace the personality God gave me and work with it.

I found green grass everywhere in my life when I finally took the time to look. It wasn't up to my husband, children, or career to make me happy. God gave me a great blueprint; I just needed to follow His guidance. I settled into motherhood much better once I started mothering within my personality, nurtured a few solid friendships, and pursued some flexible professional opportunities within the boundaries of my gifts and talents.

I'm not the Suzie Homemaker I thought I'd be. I can cook and bake with the best of the Food Channel folks, but don't ask me where the duct tape is or when my water bill is due. I just buy another roll of brightly colored tape and have the bills on automatic payment. That's me.

Instead of fighting God's design, let's start recognizing and honoring our unique, God-given personalities! After all, it's the message we've given to our children their entire lives: *You're special. God made you like no one else in the world.* However, many moms believe the complete opposite about themselves. We create in our minds an image of a "good mother" and judge ourselves on whether we live up to it. Our joy can't be found in comparison, but in living out our strengths. Laurie Wallin, certified life coach, speaker, and author of *Why Your Weirdness is Wonderful*, says it this way: "We are each given a one-of-a-kind combination of strengths, life experiences, spiritual gifts, and personality. When we're living out who God created us to be, we feel better, live better, and shine our light a lot more brightly. When we aren't, we create a vacuum that no one else can fill."[1]

> Instead of fighting God's design, let's start recognizing and honoring our unique, God-given personalities!

Certain skills and talents are always going to come easier than others. They're like breathing. Easy and energizing. Our weaknesses, on the other hand, can suck the joy and zeal right out of us. Why? Because it's difficult for us to admit that we're struggling in places of our life—especially if we believe those battles negatively affect our children in some way. Fortunately, we *can* improve and minimize the areas of struggle that compromise our effectiveness. And it's important for us to recognize that our unique characteristics and tendencies may not always be true weaknesses. After all, God created us. He made us for a unique purpose. We're all as individual as our fingerprints. Trying to be someone or something we're not simply works against God's design.

Where Are We Cooking With Gas?

So how do we move past our fears and start working within our God-given personalities? After all, that's what brings confidence and energy into our mothering. Let's highlight the positive! We're doing a lot of things well, even if it doesn't always feel like it. Talking to trusted friends may reveal strengths we didn't realize we had. An honest, personal examination can also reveal areas where we shine.

Take a personality inventory. Over the years, we've both found it incredibly enlightening to discover more about our own psychological personality profiles. For example, the Myers-Briggs Type Indicator (MBTI) personality inventory (http://myersbriggs.org) can provide insights into the way God made us. Laurie Wallin also recommends the Clifton Strengthsfinder (http://gallupstrengths center.com). When we gain a better understanding of how we're wired, this often sheds new light on our strengths and struggles.

For example, a mom who is very uncomfortable at school open houses, kids' birthday parties, and small talk in the parking lot may be more of an introvert by nature. No wonder she feels like she wants to crawl out of her skin during these times! If we feel we're working against our personalities on a regular basis, it can make for a rather nervous existence. However, that same mom—understanding the nature of introversion not as a weakness but rather a personality trait—can learn how to limit those activities for herself.

> Trying to be someone or something we're not simply works against God's design.

This introverted mom may be especially gifted at one-on-one interaction. For example, when she invites just one or two kids over for a playdate, she excels at making each child feel valued and special.

Laurie Wallin explains this well: "Our energy replenishes itself easily when we're working out of our strengths. It also erases competition. I almost never feel jealous of other people. When we appreciate our own strengths and personalities and are comfortable with ourselves, we can better appreciate the strengths of others and draw on them."[2]

Ask trusted, honest sources. We may be pleasantly surprised that others see so many positive qualities in us that we've never recognized as strengths. Asking those who love us and truly care about us will give us the most accurate and uplifting information.

Melinda

As a young mother, I was so desperate for connection that I'd take it anywhere I could find it. This sometimes led me to toxic "friends" who were competitive and subtly demeaning or judgmental. Steer clear. Nothing will make you feel more insecure in your mothering than allowing these types of people into your inner circle. Pray that God will bring women into your life who will recognize and encourage your strengths.

Examine where we feel "groovy." What are good indicators of our strengths? It's when time seems to float by and we're enjoying whatever we're doing so much that we take little notice of the clock. (By the way, neither of us feels like this when we're cleaning—although we wish we did!) It doesn't feel forced. Maybe evening snuggling went on way beyond bedtime. Three books turned into six. Those are times that can show us where we flow in mothering.

Where Are We Just Getting By?

We all have weaknesses. Comfort zones can feel very small sometimes. Insecurity creeps in and we believe that we're completely defined by these weaknesses—more than our strengths. If we believe that we all "fall short" (Romans 3:23), we know that we're broken. That's a good starting place for understanding what God calls us to do with those areas of struggle.

Lovin' Spoonful

Comparison is the thief of joy.

Unknown

Our anxiety and insecurities are often rooted in comparing ourselves, and our children, to others with very different personalities from ours.

We can also realize we're doing a good job of "getting by," but we run the risk of presenting an inaccurate image of ourselves to family and friends if we never own up to areas of struggle.

Kathy

I wanted to be a good family bookkeeper. I really did. My mom had always taught me to balance my checking account to the penny. Until I had kids, taking care of personal finances wasn't really much of a task. But over the course of the first few years of motherhood, I started having trouble paying bills on time, along with tracking spending and saving. I finally admitted to friends, family, and professionals that I was overwhelmed. I've made numerous small and large accommodations for myself to structure our finances in ways that are more congruent to my (impulsive, distracted) personality. For example, enrolling in daily notification systems for accounts helps keep a "top of the mind" awareness regarding balances and transactions.

We can't completely ignore our weaknesses. But hyperfocusing on them isn't healthy or productive, either. Instead, we have to learn how to work within them, doing as much as we can to cushion their impact both on ourselves and our families. The result is more peace and less guilt. So how do we learn to do this?

Increase Our Comfort Zones

Become proactive. Just because we'll never be completely proficient at something doesn't mean we can't do it or can't ever learn how to do it. Very often mothering requires us to do things that aren't comfortable. G. K. Chesterton said, "Anything worth doing is worth doing badly." Many things in motherhood are important, even if they don't come naturally to us. We owe it to our families to make the effort, even in areas where we don't do particularly well. We can get much stronger in an area with a little support and practice. Weaknesses are just underdeveloped strengths.

Kathy

I'll never be super tidy and organized. I've learned how to be clean enough and organized enough so that my family doesn't suffer too much from this Achilles' heel. It's the best I can do. At various times of my kids' lives, it has had a horrendous impact on their happiness and our family's well-being. Through the help of several friends and professionals, and a whole host of books on ADD, that's been my goal for over ten years. Enough is enough. More is too much. And not enough is devastating.

> We can't completely ignore our weaknesses. But hyperfocusing on them isn't healthy or productive, either.

Get help; it's not just for us. We have to remember that it's not all about us. Our family can be better served when we reach out and ask for support. Our weaknesses provide opportunities for others to help us—that is, if we let them. There's the rub. Outside help for moms can be hard to come by. There are so many barriers for moms needing help—some real, some that only exist in our minds. Mom mentors are great resources for easily accessible, peer-to-peer support and guidance. We'll talk about them in chapter 9. One way to get the help we need is to *offer* it whenever we can. It helps eliminate the guilt when we need it ourselves.

Come to Peace With Our Limits

Set boundaries. If we struggle with organization, buying twenty pairs of jeans is probably not a good idea. Keep it simple. Know where to stop—with possessions, time, and work.

Melinda

My people-pleasing tendencies have always drawn me to want to do it all. As a very young girl, I hopped onto the performance treadmill, and I kept increasing the speed as I got older, even though I never reached my destination of feeling "enough." God has brought me a long way over the years, but when I was a young mother, my marriage and family were sacrificed time and time again on the altar of my need to perform. I could tell you that it was to please God and others, and to some degree that was true. But honestly, it was mostly about me. I wanted to maintain a certain image and level of importance in others' eyes. Even if it meant my family suffered.

> Our weaknesses provide opportunities for others to help us. That is, if we let them.

This was especially damaging because I'm not a Type-A, highly organized person. No. When I get too much going, I quickly lose IQ points. My capacity to follow through on commitments without losing my marbles has always been far lower than I'd like. Eventually, I had to make a choice: sacrifice my health, mental well-being, and family, or slow down and respect the limits of my personality. When I ask Him, God shows me where my focus needs to be. That makes it much easier for me to know when to say yes and when to say no, and do it without guilt—even if other people just don't understand. My worth no longer hinges on anyone's approval. Only His. When we respect the way He made us, our whole family experiences peace.

Redefine failure. We all have a picture in our heads of what success means for a mom. For Rachel, creative prowess was key to being a good mother. For years, she tried to be "the crafty mom." She was miserable and hated every second of it. Mercy finally came in the form of a house remodel. She was forced to put all of her craft supplies and instruments into long-term storage. Her family lived in an RV where there were no stickers, knitting needles, scrapbooking papers, or elaborate stamps to remind her of her perceived internal failure. When it came time to unpack, instead of returning the craft supplies to her reinvented space, she threw them all into one of the construction dumpsters. "I finally realized it's never going to happen. It's just not me. I packed up all my good intentions and left my regret behind. It was such a powerful moment of self-acceptance. And my boys told me that they didn't even want me to be 'the crafty mom'!" says Rachel. "I decided that I wasn't a failure. It just wasn't going to be where I chose to put my energy."

Find an accountability partner. We may not have an addiction, but we need people to hold our feet to the fire. Where we need accountability may seem like small places, but these places can end up having a devastating effect on us—and by extension, our families.

Kathy

I had to give up being in charge of absolutely everything in the home. I simply couldn't do it. I wasn't doing anyone favors pretending I could. The shame of feeling inadequate was getting in the way of my family's well-being. Ben began running most of our household finances. This relieved me of the entire responsibility, and his involvement helped keep me accountable in an area of struggle for me.

Regardless of our personality types, motherhood will sometimes require us to do things that are uncomfortable and scary. It's part of

Lovin' Spoonful

We get better at doing something when we do it over and over. Research has found that it takes about 10,000 hours to become an expert—in anything. In Malcolm Gladwell's book *The Outliers*, he demonstrates this phenomenon, looking at everything from what made the Beatles so successful to why Bill Gates rose to the top.

our jobs as moms. This is where we have to lean on God's strength to push past our fear and do what's best for our children.

Melinda

My natural tendency is to avoid conflict. During my twenties, I was particularly terrified of making waves. Then Micah was born. Life became a constant flurry of doctor appointments and lab visits. Micah's doctor (Kathy's husband) told me to apply for the Early Intervention Program (EIP) immediately so Micah could begin the physical and feeding therapy that he desperately needed. I called the EIP office numerous times, politely expressing Micah's need to be seen. No response. I finally had to accept that "nice" and "polite" weren't moving my son any closer to getting help. I decided to do what seemed horrifying at the time. I showed up at the EIP office, knees knocking, and refused to leave until someone agreed to see Micah and begin his therapy. Quite bold for a shy, timid Christian girl. God gave me the courage I needed. I didn't have the strength to do it, but He did. It was only the first of many times I would have to seriously rock the boat to achieve what was needed. Each time I flexed my assertiveness muscle, it got a little easier. Since my husband has now nicknamed me "The Polecat" in these types of situations, I can assume that timidity is no longer a problem for me.

Examining strengths and weaknesses in mothering is not a one-time process. We both continually do this after twenty years of being moms. We'll probably do it in a different way when we become grandmothers! As long as we stay focused on being obedient to our calling, our journey will be fruitful. Our comfort zones can expand. Our families can benefit. We can become more accepting of who God made us.

I'm very organized and a planner, and we all know motherhood is rarely organized or planned far into the future! God has taught me so much since becoming a mama—about the differences between personality types and using it as an excuse for certain actions (like over-control, etc.). I need to allow God to use my personality to best parent the baby He has given me!

—Jenna, mother of one

Stirring Your Thoughts

1. Where do you feel like you're thriving?
2. Where do you feel like you're struggling? Name three places.
3. In looking at your struggles, rank them from one to three with one being the issue that presents the most frustration for you as a mom.
   1)
   2)
   3)
4. Looking at number one on your list of frustrations, start by brainstorming how you're currently working through this issue in your life.
5. Still working with your number one mothering frustration, use this model to explore your strengths:

   A more **"insert your name here"** way to work through **"insert #1 frustration"** would be doing it this way:

6. Complete the same for your number two frustration.

7. Complete the same for your number three frustration.

Let's Get Cookin'

- All of us have weaknesses, skillwise. We need to bring in other people to help us with these. Laurie Wallin, certified life coach, speaker, and author of *Why Your Weirdness Is Wonderful*, suggests asking the following questions of ourselves:

    Does it need to be done?

    Do I need to be the one to do it?

    If it needs to be done, how can I do it within my strengths?

    She advises finding ways to always work with who you are![3]

- Take a personality inventory. We recommend the Myers-Briggs Type Indicator (MBTI) or the Clifton Strengthsfinder. Share your results with your loved ones and use this information to tailor your approach to mothering.

- Where can you mentally transform a "failure" into an "attempt that didn't fit"? Make a decision today to let go of something that you don't want to put more money or energy into.

Chapter 5
Claiming Your Identity and Aligning Your Priorities

What needs to stay in our mothering? What needs to go? If it enriches and nourishes our families, it's worth keeping. This includes our active relationships with God and our husbands, healthy lifestyle habits, and godly friendships, to name a few. What needs to go can often be surprising. If we don't have a clear sense of what and Who guides us, we're vulnerable to unwise voices and our own volatile emotions. We have to be dependent on God's leading as life's seasons and circumstances change.

The required amount of time and energy we devote to our priorities can ebb and flow throughout motherhood. Determining our focus is a continual and prayerful process, led by the Holy Spirit. The priorities we pursue, the principles we stand for, have to be well-defined and rock solid. We must do whatever it takes to gain the knowledge and support we need to stand strong.

Just Who Do We Think We Are?

We have to know *Whose* we are in order to be confident in *who* we are. Our identity is rooted in Christ, rather than the world. Nothing can change it, not even something as monumental as motherhood.

Melinda

For my entire life, I've identified myself as a writer. In second grade I won an essay contest. The award was an adorable strawberry-shaped notebook. It was the first time I remember getting rewarded for my writing. It lit a spark inside me that propelled me through grade school and college. Over the years, my writing has always brought me consistent ego-boosting accolades and recognition.

In early motherhood, I drove myself to great extremes because I felt much of my worth and value depended on my writing or performing in some way. My family suffered. Micah's illness was clarifying for me. God made it clear that I had to arrange my writing pursuits around my family's needs instead of vice versa. My writing career has been up, down, completely dormant, and everything in between as I've raised my children. It's never made sense to operate this way—from the world's perspective. I should've *always* been making more money. This is still the case today! Yet through the years, God has always provided. And my oldest is now eighteen. I feel a great sense of peace as I follow the Holy Spirit's leading in this area. As I began drawing closer to God, I experienced a growing assurance and revelation of His very real love for *me*, not my talents or what I could produce. He continues to reveal the depth of His love to me daily. I'll always love to write, but it's not where the focus of my identity is anymore.

> We have to know **Whose** we are in order to be confident in **who** we are.

In Galatians 2:20, Paul says, "It is no longer I who live, but Christ who lives in me. And the life I now live in the flesh I live by faith in the Son of God" (ESV). Since we believe this is true, we know we're *not* our own. How many times have we thought, *I feel like I've lost myself in being a mom?* Isn't it reassuring to know that's not possible? We can't lose our identity. It's eternally secure in the hands of the Savior who died to purchase it. Rest assured, we may lose our keys, our kids' soccer uniforms, and even our minds from time to time, but we can never lose who we are in Christ.

However, if we believe our identity is formed by us alone—our achievements, our circumstances, and our productivity and usefulness to others—we're bound to feel unstable. When the foundation of our personhood is Christ-based, we're much more resilient and confident in our roles and choices as mothers. We can quit worrying about what other people think of us. His opinion becomes the only one that matters. If we look for our sense of self by pursuing the goals our culture tells us are valuable, we'll never end our search. And we'll never measure up. They use a different yardstick—one that's always changing, by the way. God's high value of us is unchanging and eternal. Our talents, unique personality traits, preferences, and gifts all come from our Creator. They're a part of who we are, and they don't determine our worth or value.

Making the Hard Choices

Motherhood is clearly honored by God. It was His idea! God is choosing this life, this family, this time for His purpose through us. Small yet significant hard choices often lead to those moments that our children remember and that we treasure. It's the decision to play Polly Pockets on the floor with our five-year-old rather than succumb to the calling of the couch. It's the choice to watch our child play

 Lovin' Spoonful

Priority Prayer for Moms

Dear Lord, thank You for all of my blessings: for my family, my home, the very food on my table. Help me to see my life as You see it, created for Your glory and the purposes of Your heart. Help me to be wise in my choices as I care for Your children and my family. Amen.

soccer or baseball on cold, hard bleachers when we'd rather just stay home and get some things done. Everyone wins when we choose to be there when our kids *want* us instead of just when they *need* us.

Through her website and ministry, Shaping Your Identity in Motherhood, author Linda Bernson-Tang encourages moms to make the decision to maximize these small moments with our children. "Our presence and involvement, even in little things, says, 'You're important.' It's building relationship not just for today, but for so many more tomorrows," says Bernson-Tang. "So often we see our child playing or watching a show and think, *This is a great opportunity to get something else done,* or *Great, I could really use the break,* instead of joining in with them."

> How many times have we thought, **I feel like I've lost myself in being a mom?** Isn't it reassuring to know that's not possible?

It's impossible to do this every time. We understand that. As they get further from kindergarten and closer to high school graduation, we have more energy to make these choices. Our perspective changes as we move out of those early years. "My kids are ten and eight now, and I realized that my time left with them is finite. It inspires me to be more intentional about not missing opportunities to just be with them," says Linda.[1]

When we talk to our families, we may get a surprising picture of just how joyfully we are (or are not) embracing these opportunities.

Melinda

I received such a wake-up call in December 2000. I had just written our annual Christmas letter. My upbeat and glowing descriptions of our family life, sweet children, and their adorable accomplishments made the Means family leap off the page. Before I shared our joy with the world, I gave my husband the final copy to read.

He began reading and then chuckled.

"Why are you laughing?" I asked, a bit annoyed.

"I'm sorry," he said. "It's just that I got to the part where you say how much you *enjoy* being a mom. It doesn't really seem like it sometimes." *Ouch.*

"Really? Why do you say that?" I responded (through clenched teeth).

"Well, you just always seem so stressed out," he said.

I couldn't argue. As a young mother, I was often frustrated and angry. I lashed out at my children when they, simply by being children, impeded my progress on some household task or made it difficult for me to concentrate when I was writing articles. I'd think, *If they'd be less demanding, I'd get so much more done. I'd be so much less stressed.* My heart hurts when I think back on that time.

Through this enlightening conversation with my husband, Micah's illness, and other events in my life, God slowly and graciously brought me to a realization that radically changed the real problem with my mothering: my attitude. Writing and home management *were* my responsibilities. However, as soon as I became a mother, my children were the preeminent and primary responsibility He had given me, outside of my marriage. My children were *not* the interruptions. The other demands on my time and energy were what had to be tamed in order to give my most precious assets the attention they deserved.

Taming the other responsibilities outside of our families can seem overwhelming. Here are some practical tips:

Gain a long-term perspective. Nothing lasts forever. Every stage and season in a child's life is temporary. The demands continually ebb and flow. For example, when we have toddlers and feel we may never get a relaxed moment—or even a moment alone—we can look forward a year or two. This can feel almost impossible with our first child. We might not be able to envision what life will be like in a year or two. But our moms can. Or friends who have older children. Talking to them can help us to gain a long-term perspective. When we're frustrated and struggling because we aren't accomplishing certain objectives (like going back to school—or just getting our hair colored), we can take comfort in knowing that these things will become not only possible, but also much easier, later on.

Kathy

My youngest is now eleven. When my oldest was eleven, my other children were nine, six, and three. What I'm able to do now versus then is vastly different. The struggles are different, but so are the opportunities. From 1995 to 1997, I couldn't have cooked dinner without Barney the dinosaur. My oldest son told me once, "Of course that lady on TV can cook dinner in thirty minutes or less—there's no babies running around!"

> Everyone wins when we choose to be there when our kids **want** us, instead of just when they **need** us.

Accept "less than perfect." For some of us, this is the most difficult aspect of motherhood. From the house and laundry to how we're perceived by those around us, perfectionism can handicap our mothering lives. Keep it as basic and simple as possible. The laundry still needs to be done, the house still needs to be cleaned, and bills still need to be paid. However, we can lower our expectations, simplify, and delegate some of these tasks.

Helping others is wonderful—but family first. Ministry to others and volunteering are honorable, but not when we pour more energy into helping others than we do into the well-being of those closest to us. We've both been guilty of this. Why do we do this? Well, honestly, strangers often seem to appreciate the acts of kindness more! And it makes us look good and feel worthwhile. In her book *A Woman After God's Own Heart*, Elizabeth George writes about a time when she realized she was putting others before her family:

> Katherine and Courtney wanted to know who the food was for. I lowered the beautifully arranged tray to their level and took advantage of this opportunity to teach them about Christian giving.

I explained, "Mrs. X has had a baby, and we're taking dinner to her family so she can rest after being in the hospital."

That sounded good until my own children asked, "What are we having for dinner?" When I said that we were having macaroni and cheese with hot dogs (again!), I was sharply convicted of my wrong priorities. I had put someone else, Mrs. X, ahead of my own family.[2]

> Priorities are not reflected by our words, but by our actions.

Having purpose, being productive . . . yes, these are important virtues worth pursuing. However, they need to undergo a redefinition in the context of motherhood. After a busy day with kids and other responsibilities, how many times have we looked at our wrecked houses and endless to-do lists and thought, *I haven't stopped working, but I haven't gotten a thing done!* That's a lie. We have to redefine *productive.* Providing for our families, tending to skinned knees, having conversations about Jesus as we cart kids to and from school—those are worthy investments.

Lovin' Spoonful

Wisdom From the Bible About Priorities

Commit to the Lord whatever you do, and he will establish your plans.

Proverbs 16:3

Do not conform to the pattern of the world, but be transformed by the renewing of your mind. Then you will be able to test and approve what God's will is—his good, pleasing and perfect will.

Romans 12:2

Move It to the Back Burner or Turn Up the Heat?

Motherhood requires us to do an inventory of what's essential versus what's superficial. Our time and resources are precious. What should we spend them on?

Earlier in the chapter we talked about identity. Our assurance of our value in Christ is the very engine that drives our choices and provides us with guidance. It has to be cultivated through regular time with God. We explore practical ways to make this possible in depth in chapter 13. Certainly, our marriages deserve regular quality time and energy, but we also need to take care of our own physical well-being by getting adequate sleep (to the extent that's possible!) and making healthy lifestyle choices. This enables us to better meet the demands of motherhood. Godly friendships will also support us in our roles as moms. They'll help us maintain perspective when life gets chaotic and messy.

The areas of our lives that need to be temporarily shuffled to the back burner in motherhood are different from mom to mom. They vary depending on the age of our children, our circumstances at any given moment, and the unique demands of our family relationships.

 Lovin' Spoonful

According to Merriam-Webster, *margin* can be defined as "an extra amount of something (such as time or space) that can be used if it is needed."[3]

For moms, this means embracing the reality that having children means unpredictability and continually being able to switch plans. This means not packing our schedules so full that any variation sends us into a meltdown. Pray each day that God will help you know what the most important things are for you to accomplish each day.

Only we can decide which to place on a back burner and which to bring to a full boil. Our job is to be obedient and flexible, not fixated on doing *everything* we want to do *all* the time.

It's important to examine our own personal threshold for activity and plan accordingly. Why is this so important? Because we're human. When we're overwhelmed, cranky, and stressed, it fans out and infects the entire home environment. The stress goes viral. And that's not good for anyone. So many of us have been in the situation where we know something's got to give, but how do we decide what those things are? Aren't we supposed to be able to "have it all" these days?

Different stages and seasons require us to recalibrate and evaluate. Sometimes God calls us to step back from or adjust our responsibilities during motherhood. Other times He calls us to move forward, which can sometimes be just as uncomfortable.

Kathy

The year was 2009. My fourth child was in first grade. After years of struggle, I had finally found a few solid friendships and was receiving adequate help from a variety of resources. I felt like I could take a long sigh of relief. I deserved it, didn't I? It took me almost two years to exhale.

God had a different, yet equally sweet, plan. He was stirring something in my heart I could no longer ignore. I had made it through a lonely struggle that He didn't want other mothers to experience. What was I going to do about it? I was not ready to answer God's call wholeheartedly like Isaiah: "The Lord [said], 'Whom shall I send? And who will go for us?' And I said, 'Here am I. Send me!'" (Isaiah 6:8).

Instead, I prayed something along the lines of: "Here I am, Lord. I am tired, Lord. Please stop calling me in the night. I just got some decent sleep, Lord. I'm hanging out here for a while. Your people will be fine."

Others agreed with me. God, however, was leading me toward taking those years and experiences to help other moms. "Can't I just enjoy my kids, Lord?" His answer? "Sure! But get cracking on taking care of some of the 'least of these' among you—the struggling moms. They're some of the vulnerable ones that I treasure. Build them up. Show them how much I love them and let them know about my mercy and grace. You promised me, remember?"

Mothering From Scratch, both the blog and the book, was born from obedience to that calling. It still feels uncomfortable at times. I'm incredibly flawed and sometimes far from a confident mother. My kids have made adjustments as I've pursued this venture. So has my husband. My availability is still present, but God's calling has changed some of the nuances of how I mother. His grace is abundant. His mercy endures. That's a very good thing.

What Goes in the Trash?

As we redefine our identity in Christ, change our priorities, and make adjustments, the Holy Spirit brings character issues and "hidden" emotional and spiritual struggles to the surface. (They're never really hidden, are they? We only think they are!) As God opens our eyes to these issues, we need to submit them to Him and follow His leading in each area. They can include entitlement, negativity, a critical spirit, comparison/jealousy, people pleasing, depression, and anxiety. These are the heart issues—the internal struggles that keep us from being healthy and at peace, the ones that negatively affect our ability to mother with passion and purpose. Addressing these issues is nearly always uncomfortable and painful. Unfortunately, we can't provide the solution to all those struggles in this chapter. Whole books have been written on each of those issues! In some cases, we may require significant help to haul out this sort of trash, especially if it's heavy.

Melinda

As I've mentioned earlier in the book, one of the major issues that motherhood brought to the surface in my life was people pleasing. During early motherhood, an internal battle was waging inside me when I had people telling me, "You have so many talents. You need

to use them." My own mind was saying, *You need to be important!*
You need the money! And my people-pleasing nature wanted to
satisfy those voices. On the other hand, I just wanted to be a good,
relaxed mommy. I longed to have enough margin in my life that
the time and attention I gave to my children didn't stress me out.
Building margin isn't easy as a people pleaser. God has brought me
a long way. Seeking godly counseling and committing to move past
people pleasing—one decision at a time, with God's help—has been
key to getting healthier. I still struggle, but I'm no longer running
on a perpetual performance treadmill in order to feel important.

Here's the real bottom line: Motherhood does change our priorities. It requires us to stretch and adjust our lives in ways that are
beautiful. However, it can be so easy to live in a sort of survival mode,
making these decisions on a wing and a prayer. It's worthwhile to
take time and find courage to examine why we're doing whatever
we're doing and how we're doing it. Priorities aren't reflected by
our words, but by our actions. Once we gain security in our true
identity through our relationship with Jesus, He helps us make those
tough choices. The closer we are to Him, the clearer they become.

I am getting better at saying no, but it's still hard to do, especially
when you feel like something will suffer if you do say no. God will
always provide the right person for the task, and sometimes that
person is just waiting for an opportunity but doesn't take it because
you keep beating them to the punch.

—Tina, mother of two

Stirring Your Thoughts

1. How do you think our culture views having and raising children? What tells you this?
2. "Children are a heritage from the Lord, offspring a reward
   from him" (Psalm 127:3). Based on this verse, how does God
   view your children?

3. When you bear God's view of your children in mind, how can that change your approach or attitude about mothering?

4. What are some blessings in your life that are a direct result of making some hard choices in mothering?

5. List three invisible sacrifices you've made or are making for your children. You know, the ones no one else sees or fully appreciates. What fruit do you hope to see from these?

Let's Get Cookin'

- Below is a list of common life priorities. Circle five or six that you consider your highest priorities at this time in your life and then rank them.

  Hobbies   Relationship with God

  Career   Church Involvement

  Education Childcare

  Wealth   Children's Education

  Self-Care   Relationships With Others

  Marriage   Extended Family Relationships

  Volunteer Work   Other _____

- Do your life choices reflect the priorities you've circled? If not, name three small but tangible changes you can make to move closer to reflecting these priorities in your daily actions. Do you sense God wants you to change the order of these priorities? Ask Him to give you the wisdom and courage to do so.

- Find one small moment this week to say yes to something with your child when you'd rather say no.

Chapter 6

Good News: Your Future Won't Spoil

It's been said that dreams are like a window to our soul. Whether we recognize it or not, God has placed dreams in our hearts that reflect His unique purpose for us. As a mom, do *you* have a dream in your heart? Do you feel like you'll *never* have the time or energy to fully pursue it? Is it buried under loads of laundry or lost in the shuffle of the workplace or other responsibilities? We were once mommies of young ones. We've been there. We remember it well. Moms all over the world are in your same shoes.

Perhaps you're not completely content in your job. Or maybe you're a stay-at-home mom who loves her children but dreams of one day becoming an entrepreneur or otherwise working outside the home. Or you might be working toward your dream but you feel like it's moving incredibly slowly. Finances, time, and a lack of other resources can feel like barriers as we're raising our families.

We want to offer you hope. As mothers, we'll *always* have our talents, intellect, and aspirations. They don't become obsolete or grow less useful. They won't spoil. On the other hand, children are more like ripe little berries freshly picked in the sun. When their time is here, it's here. When it's gone, so are they. How do we foster the dreams in our own hearts as we're tending to the hearts and needs of our children? It's an important and sometimes difficult question. However, it's not impossible for us to dig deeper and come out with what we can do today to follow our dreams.

Surrendering to God's Plan

Most of us like to quantify our progress and see a straight line to our goals. In motherhood, we can experience lots of zigs, zags, ups, and downs as we're pursuing the dreams that God has placed in our hearts. Taking the time to write down our priorities, goals, and dreams both inside and outside of motherhood will help give us a map. Writing them down on paper serves as a reminder when we get off track and/or become weary and overwhelmed by life. Make these lists prayerfully. Ask God to guide your thoughts and heart toward Him.

> As mothers, we'll **always** have our talents, intellect, and aspirations. . . . They won't spoil.

Our age or the age of our children doesn't always determine when we'll pursue goals outside of motherhood. Relying on the leading of the Holy Spirit, we'd be wise to take a careful, regular assessment of our priorities, dreams/goals, and life circumstances. For example, once our last child is in school, there can be an immediate pressure to somehow do more than what we've been doing. Some believe that the hardest phase of child-rearing is over. In fact, it's often just an enormous shift in our role as a mom.

Melinda

When my kids were young, I started formulating my path to my dreams based on the priorities that I believed God had given me for my life. If someone asked me to do something, I would refer back

Lovin' Spoonful

A Prayer of Surrender for Moms

Lord, here I am.
All of me.
All my desires, dreams, and ambitions. Make them Yours.
I trust in Your wisdom. I give You my heart, my mind, and my soul.
Amen.

to that priority list and ask myself, "Is this a good time to pursue this opportunity? Does it make sense with my written priorities?" At times, I said no to things that would've furthered my dream but been a drain on my family.

I found that just because my last child started school and I had more time, the realization of my dream didn't happen as soon as I thought it would. For years, I had worked as a part-time freelance writer for various healthcare companies. It was not the writing I dreamed of doing, but it was where the opportunities were for me at the time. And it was profitable. We needed the money. When my kids were ten and seven I thought I now had the time to branch out from health care into writing for Christian magazines, which my heart longed to do. I started a parenting blog and began to write for some national Christian publications.

I thought I could go full speed ahead. And then my daughter hit middle school. I entered a very difficult season of parenting that required an incredible amount of energy and focus. I had a choice to make. So I put my dream on the back burner and concentrated on her; my daughter ranked above what I was personally pursuing at that time. Surprisingly, I felt relief when I pulled back on my dream. I had the sense that God was calling me to put my dreams on pause—He was not asking me to hit Stop and quit moving ahead forever. For me, this was the key to feeling peace instead of resentment.

Kathy

When the last of my four children started school, I was often asked, "What are you going to do *now*?" I felt pressure to do more, produce more, *be* more somehow. But, personally, I simply needed to get ready for the next phase of mothering.

We know we're not alone in this. You may be thinking about the difficult season you're in and wondering if you'll ever be able to actively pursue your dream. We like what Cindi McMenamin says about surrendering our plans to God in her book *When a Woman Discovers Her Dream*:

> We often have our own image of what the dream will look like, how we'll get it, and when. Yet Proverbs 16:3 says, "Commit your works to the Lord and your plans will be established." It doesn't say plan out your way, move full speed ahead, and expect God to follow. . . . Hold them [your plans] with an open hand and say, as Jesus said to His heavenly Father in the Garden . . . "Not my will, but Yours be done." . . . That's the kind of heart we need to have before we can truly live out our dream.[1]

You may feel like Renee, who had a passion for sewing. When her youngest child was a baby, she attended a sewing guild meeting, where she listened to a meaningful-to-her speaker. Renee shares, "The speaker was a fabric designer. As I listened to her, I remember breathing a prayer, 'God, I would love to be a fabric designer someday.' With three small kids, I couldn't fathom how or when that would ever happen." However, she admits that at times she definitely tried too hard to make things come to pass. And it never worked in her timing or through forcing it. "Each time a new opportunity came, it really was the hand of God. Doors would open unexpectedly," she says. "Once, at a trade show, I was in an elevator and struck up a conversation with a man who happened to be the president of a fabric company, and who needed a designer. And I got the job, even though I hadn't really designed fabric before. He took a chance on me. I could never have orchestrated that meeting."

Today, Renee is living out her dream as a freelance designer for a variety of fabric companies. She even sells some of her paintings on the side. How in the world can this happen? It does. God orchestrates things we could never imagine would happen.

How can we know we're pursuing our dreams in accordance with God's will? This will be a personal journey for each of us, but here are a few practical questions we can ask ourselves:

Are we being deliberate about our walk with Christ first? What does this even look like? How do we put Christ first in our lives? Do we have a deliberate, daily time in prayer and in the Word? Are we surrendering to the Holy Spirit and cultivating a teachable heart? Do we surround ourselves with the body of Christ regularly in church, Bible study, or small groups? Pursuing our dreams outside of a vibrant relationship with Jesus is foolish and futile.

Danielle, a mother of four, now has her own thriving freelance photography business. But she was once a mom of young children who felt called to walk away from her job in the corporate world. The time between leaving that job and fully pursuing her dream of photography was much longer than she had expected. However, she said her intimate relationship with the Lord allowed her to be peaceful as her dream slowly unfolded. "I am so thankful that I had that closeness with Christ because it enabled me to trust Him, His financial provision, and His timing."

Years ago, Danielle heard author Elisabeth Elliot pose a couple of questions that resonated with her for years. Elliot asked, "What are you living for? How do you accomplish it?" Danielle shares: "She went on to say that when we view our goals and dreams in the light of eternity, it changes the whole equation. God's plan for us and the choices He leads us to make can be very different from what seems important, successful, and logical according to the world." We encourage you to view your dreams from an eternal perspective.

Lovin' Spoonful

Moses didn't see the burning bush until he was forty. Sarah was in her nineties when she gave birth to a nation. Mother Teresa didn't receive her call to minister to the poor of Calcutta until she was thirty-six. Take heart. Time hasn't run out for you. Where do you have the hardest time believing that God will fulfill your dream?

Are we pursuing the dream at someone else's expense? Of course, we're talking about our children. But we would also suggest evaluating the impact on our husbands, relationships, extended family, and/or other areas of ministry. The world says it should *always* be our turn; we should *always* be at the front of the line. What did Jesus say? "The last will be first, and the first will be last" (Matthew 20:16).

Danielle also shares some valuable advice she received that she now shares with other young mothers whom she mentors: "May I never be a hero to strangers and a stranger to my children."

Is God beginning to open doors that we can't open ourselves?

Melinda

When my middle school crisis had subsided, I began to feel a peace and a physical and creative energy I hadn't felt for a long time. I went to another writing conference and the floodgates began to open. Before that, I felt like I was beating my head against a wall. Suddenly He opened doors that I could never have orchestrated on my own.

So let us ask you. What does this look like for you? What doors do you want to see God open? If we don't dream it and write it down, we will likely never see it happen and be able to give God the glory for it.

How Do We Know If Our Dream Is a Good Fit?

It's not only important to examine whether it's the right time for the pursuit of our dreams. We must also discern if it's a good fit and if it's congruent with our values, our families, and our circumstances. How do we know?

As we pursue any passion outside of mothering, we need to examine whether it's fruitful or wasteful. *Time. Money. Energy.* Those are all valuable gifts. We need to be frugal with how we expend them. When we choose activities that continually deplete our resources to dangerously low levels, the price is not paid by us alone. Our families take the brunt of the hit. If our relationships are being harmed by our ambition, then the good of personal achievement actually hurts others. Is that a true, authentic sign of God's will? How can we know if we're hurting our families in the process of pursuing the things we enjoy? What is a good, safe middle ground?

> If we don't dream it and write it down, we will likely never see it happen and be able to give God the glory for it.

Let's go back to Danielle's story for a moment. Danielle is a gifted photographer who has the opportunity to pursue a profitable niche in wedding photography. However, Friday through Saturday night is her own prime family time. "It's the time I get to spend with my husband and be a part of my teenage children's sporting events." For now, she's chosen to concentrate on family photography, which is more flexible. It sounds simple, but this is a courageous way of approaching her passions and dreams with others in mind.

As we consider how to use the talents God's given us, we're wise to be sensitive to God's leading regarding how we can best blend our dreams with our family lives.

Kathy

When I opened an interior decorating business, my children were much younger and all four of them needed me. All. The. Time.

Now when I announce that I need to work on *Mothering From Scratch*, they say, "Okay. We'll try to be quiet." Crazy, huh? They're old enough to respect my venture and not feel ignored. It makes sense to them, and especially my husband, that I'm in a ministry that focuses on helping other moms. It wasn't always like that with my other ventures. From the start of this ministry, I discussed it with my family, asked their input, and received their blessing. I keep them informed and involved. Because my husband is a pediatrician, my ministry to mothers is almost like an extension of the family business. He ministers to kids. I feel led to help mothers. The difference is I'm not fitting my family around my dream. I'm fitting my dream around my family. They feel honored and appreciated, not neglected.

Another sign of affirmation of a godly fit can be sincere, genuine encouragement from our family. My family felt neglected when I was busy at someone else's house—on a ladder hanging *their* family photos in an attractive montage—during *my* family's dinner hour. If we experience too much pushback or not enough encouragement from those closest to us, it might be time to look back at our priority lists.

This will look different for each individual, but you can do this, too! We've found that finding the right fit includes a prayerful pursuit of priorities, as well as honest talks with family members and the formulation of clear boundaries. Set limits to protect family time and stick to them. We keep each other accountable in this area. For example, we try to get most of our writing done during school hours. But we accommodate our kids' sometimes unpredictable schedules. Limits can change based on our current life circumstances, the ages of our children, and what's happening in our families at different stages.

Each family and situation is unique. Significant issues and/or conflicts within our family relationships may need to be addressed before we can start chasing after our dreams. Marital problems, unresolved childhood issues, difficult challenges with children—such as chronic illness or learning disabilities—need to be addressed.

Personally, we have had to confront all of these issues in our own lives and families. As we did, the paths to our dreams became more wide open.

Wait? Wait? Yes, No, or Maybe

Our society is all about instant gratification. Waiting is so . . . old school. We have the "right" to be happy all the time, right? Ironically, we were never more *unhappy* than when we were pursuing personal ventures at our family's expense. We realized that although self-denial wasn't popular, it was necessary at the time for the health of our families.

As we discussed earlier, God may at times call us to put our dreams and ambitions on hold—on a shelf, if you will—for another time. We realize that this can be difficult, and not a popular thought. Rest assured, the season of hands-on mothering will end. We're wise to maximize the short window we have to guide and influence our children before it closes, all the while remembering that our dreams and ambitions don't have an expiration date. Ecclesiastes 3:1 assures us, "There is a time for everything, and a season for every activity under the heavens."

Melinda

This was a concept that didn't compute for me as a young mommy. When I had a two-year-old daughter, I thought I had come up with the perfect project to combine my writing career and motherhood. My heart and passion has always been with mothers. So, naturally, I started a family magazine. I nearly singlehandedly wrote, designed, and edited a monthly thirty-two-page publication. My business partner handled advertising, printing, and distribution.

Just as the first issue was about to launch I got some very important news. *I was pregnant.* The thought never occurred to me that perhaps there might be a slightly *better* time to pursue my dream of rocking the writing world. And maybe, just maybe, I should've realized that perhaps I hadn't cornered the market on mothering wisdom, considering I'd been on the job for a whopping two years.

But no. I went to my partner, told her I was pregnant, and then in all seriousness, said these words: "I just want you to know that I'm fully committed to our partnership and this family magazine. The new baby will not affect that commitment."

I cringe when I think back to that time and my insistence on forging full speed ahead, without regard to the cost to my family and my own well-being. It took a full year for me to absorb the insanity of it all. Here I was telling families to put family first, while my own family was faltering under the stress and time commitment of producing a magazine for families. *Irony, anyone?*

> We're wise to maximize the short window we have to guide and influence our children before it closes.

"On hold" periods or times when our dreams aren't progressing like we thought they would can seem like wasted time. But often God uses various life experiences and difficulties to give us the tools we need to run after our dreams with abandon—later. While we can easily view our children as barriers to our productivity, they're often what God uses more than anything else in our lives to strengthen us, humble us, and shape our character.

When the time is right, He will often move more boldly and miraculously than we ever thought possible. Like the loaves and the fishes, He multiplies our resources and effectiveness.

So What Can We Do to Keep Our Dreams Fresh?

Learn. As you have time, educate yourself about the things you're dreaming of. What do you need to do now to start moving in the direction of your dreams? Do you need to take a class, set aside a block of writing time, hire a sitter while you do some research, or talk with others who are already living the dream you have? You'll be ahead of the game when the time comes to pursue it.

Melinda

I went to writing conferences and workshops and read books and magazines about publishing and blogging. At the time, I could put very little of that knowledge into practice. But when the time came, I was educated and ready to hit the ground running. What can you do today to move toward your dream?

> When the time is right, He will often move more boldly and miraculously than we ever thought possible.

Break your whole dream down into parts. Regardless of your dream, it can be broken down into doable parts that you may begin pursuing. As a young mom, Renee, the fabric designer, worked craft shows, selling dolls and angels she had made. Then she began selling the patterns for these crafts at fabric stores. Renee recalls, "As my kids grew up, I also had opportunities to write a few craft books, usually late at night after all the kids were in bed."

Photographer Danielle took pictures of her family and of kids at many sporting events. Then she gave the parents photos of their children. "I called it 'The Ministry of the Bleachers,' which led to opportunities to witness to some of them."

Both of these moms followed God's leading in using their talents, establishing relationships, and building a foundation for when the time was right to more fully go after their dreams. What will it take for you to pursue parts of your dream as you move into pursuing the whole dream? Will you begin today to ask God how He wants you to proceed?

Be productive, not exhausted. As moms, we need to accept and enjoy the season we are in right now without wearing ourselves out trying to accomplish it all in a day. Enjoy your kids. Live in *this* moment.

These can be hard statements to hear when we're bored, impatient, and mired in unglamorous tasks. However, we have to remember: This is for *now,* not forever.

Melinda

I was overwhelmed by the enormity of working part time, pursuing my writing dreams, and caring for two young children, one of whom had a chronic illness. I needed permission to relax and slow down so I could take care of myself and enjoy my children. I wish someone had given this to me years ago.

Our dreams will keep. Time with our children is short and fleeting. Only God can help us keep this perspective at the forefront of our minds if we become impatient and weary in our roles as moms. Along the way, we both shared our dreams with others who reaffirmed them and encouraged us. Can you think of at least one person who can be your cheerleader as you follow God's leading?

Be assured of this: As you live out God's purpose for you, He *will* enable you to do that in a way that blends well with your mothering. It doesn't mean it will always be easy. But it's possible. He loves you unconditionally and always desires your ultimate eternal happiness. When your heart belongs to Him, so do your

Lovin' Spoonful

Even if you don't quite know what your dreams are, God does. He will awaken them in your heart at the proper time. Ephesians 2:10 tells us, "For we are God's handiwork, created in Christ Jesus to do good works, which God prepared in advance for us to do." Ask God to help you to explore your dreams. How will you put them where you can see them often? How will you live today in light of your dreams?

dreams. Trust Him. He sees you. You're not forgotten. Seek His face. He'll show it to you. Ask for the desires of your heart. He'll listen.

When I was twenty-six years old, with two baby boys, the Lord planted a seed in my heart to teach women about the Lord, His Word, and His ways. I had two more babies, and the seed grew. I taught Bible studies, attended conferences, and read books. I ached to do so much more. Last spring, in the most miraculous way, He let me know, "Now. It's time. Go." I see His reasons and better plan for the timing of fulfillment: in my marriage, in the lives of my (now) grown children, with how God is working in and through them, and in me as a wiser, more Spirit-led, and hopefully more humble woman who loves Jesus with all her heart.

—Diane, mother of four

Stirring Your Thoughts

1. What did you want to be when you were a little girl? How has that changed? How is it still the same?

2. If you could wave a magic wand, how would you change your work environment—whether at home or in the workplace?

3. Where would you like to be in . . .
   Five years?
   Ten years?

4. Do a sixty-second brainstorm. What are three unrealized life dreams you've always had for yourself?

5. How can you use your gifts and passions in smaller ways as you're waiting for bigger opportunities?

6. How has motherhood changed your dreams? How has it shaped them in ways you didn't expect?

7. How can you keep resentment from growing when you feel like life and opportunities are passing you by?

Let's Get Cookin'

- **Resolve to get more Jesus in your life.** We can do nothing without Him. Pray, read, listen as much as you can during your busy days. Commit to spending time with Him daily—even if it starts with just five minutes.

- **Make a list of priorities.** Take your time and ask God to guide your heart and thoughts. Here are some examples to get you started: Marriage, Church Involvement, Physical Health, Time with Children, Community Involvement, Scripture Study, Availability for Children, Personal Emotional Health.

  Also, prayerfully make a list of goals and dreams for both inside and outside motherhood. Pray that God will make your heart open if He wants to change your goals and dreams over time.

- **Have a discussion with your family.** Find out what they think about what you're currently pursuing outside of your current job and/or motherhood. Ask them for any ideas they might have about how you can modify what you're doing without adversely affecting your family.

- **Over the next thirty days, pick one small step to complete toward achieving a dream.** For example, research a topic you're curious about, a potential career change, or a new skill you want to learn.

Sifting It All Out

Chapter 7

Working With What
Your Mama Gave You

Our mothers influence how we mother. We can't deny it. Not a single one of us had a perfect childhood. But even if we have a good, healthy relationship with our mothers, we still may want to dig a little deeper into how our upbringing and that relationship affects our mothering today.

Whether we recognize it or not, our tendency is to do what we know—even those of us who so desperately want to be different from the mother we had.

Examining our relationships with our mothers will benefit us in a number of important ways. It can help us to recognize and be grateful for all of the positive things they gave us. Through the Holy Spirit, this often leads to extending grace to them in a way we may not have been able to do before. This journey may also bring buried anger, resentment, and bitterness to the surface, where we can confront it and allow God to bring us to a place of healing and forgiveness. We'll begin by sharing about our relationships with our mothers.

Melinda

My grandmother died when my mother was just six years old, and then my mom's father had very little contact with her during her growing-up years. On top of that, she was raised by an emotionally abusive aunt. Hope showed up in the form of my godly great-grandmother, a sweet Quaker lady who introduced my mom to Jesus. Yet the scars of my mom's childhood traumas were deep and lasting. She struggled with untreated mental illness nearly her entire life. As a mother and wife, she had difficulty being nurturing and emotionally available. Even still, I never doubted that she loved me.

It's amazing. She had these very screwed-up behaviors and thought patterns, and yet she had a very pure faith in God. It's a miracle, really. While she fought her own personal demons, she, along with my dad, taught Sunday school and brought my sister and me to church each week. She was driven by her deep love for Jesus, combined with her desire to feel worthy and "enough." My mom was always doing. Always going. I rarely saw her truly rest, either mentally or physically. Even though I brought a lot of her amazing faith into my mothering, I also adopted her "hamster on a wheel" drive.

 Lovin' Spoonful

Your responsibility is to grieve and forgive so that way you may be healed of whatever your mother might have done wrong. Then, as you see and take responsibility for your side of the problem, you will be able to receive what you did not get, gain control, and change those areas where life hasn't worked for you thus far. In this twofold process of forgiveness and responsibility, you will find unlimited growth.

from *The Mom Factor* by
Drs. Henry Cloud and John Townsend[1]

98

Kathy

I grew up with a mother who treasured and enjoyed motherhood. She felt it was the most important job on the earth. She was a blissful, stay-at-home mother in the '60s and early '70s. Later, due to divorce, she became a single mother, sometimes working two or three jobs to make ends meet. All the while, she still made me dresses and loved homemaking. When I was nine, she married my stepfather. This helped her become more of the full-time homemaker she enjoyed being. Their marriage lasted thirty-two years until his death. Theirs was a strong example of enduring, sacrificial love.

From watching her example and attitude toward mothering, I had an idealized image of what motherhood was going to be like. But when I had my children, I quickly realized that I wasn't as content as I thought I was going to be. Yes, she instilled in me a love of children that I appreciate to this day. But I had to figure out a way to make motherhood gel with my personality.

When I hear my mother's words come out of my mouth, I sometimes laugh. When I do things that she does or did when I was little, I realize that I had a rich tradition of motherhood to draw upon. I'm forever grateful. She has always been supportive of everything I have done, from attending college, to having four children, to co-writing this book. Really, my contribution to this book is a result of her wisdom and experience traveling through another generation.

It's important for us to look at our mothers with sensitive, empathetic eyes. At the same time, we also have to be willing to recognize the areas where they may have fallen short. The trick is to avoid viewing our moms with rose-colored glasses or with an unforgiving microscope.

Where Does This Relationship Show Up in Our Mothering?

The influence of our mothers can surface in all sorts of daily events and circumstances. Emotional responses influence our actions and reactions. This can be both positive and negative.

Kathy

Growing up, I always felt very loved when my mom cooked and baked for me. Somehow the warmth of the kitchen wrapped around my little-girl heart. When she worked outside of the home, I could always find something on the counter waiting for me after school. It was her way of saying "I love you." I have such warm memories of cooking with my mom. A teenager doesn't argue with a woman handing her delicious baked goods. It was her secret weapon. Problems were solved by "a good steak and potato." Chocolate chip cookies could restore hope to the world.

I use the same (manipulation) strategy with my children. When life gets tough, I get cooking. A bad day at school can be cured by the whiff of cookies baking when my children walk through the door. A case of the grumpies doesn't stand a chance against freshly baked bread. Maybe this is why I still find great stress relief in cooking and baking. It reminds me of being a nurtured kid.

> The trick is to avoid viewing our moms with rose-colored glasses or with an unforgiving microscope.

Melinda

At times, a behavior or stage in our children can open up an old wound or insecurity that we don't want our own children to experience. We want to redeem our past. This isn't all bad. But we have to be conscious of doing it in healthy, God-led ways.

I was a late bloomer. During my middle school years, I was downright unfortunate looking. You might be thinking, *Oh, yes, honey, everyone was awkward at that age.* Trust me. I had a face that truly only a mother could love.

And my mother did love me. However, she didn't provide me with much guidance in regard to makeup, hair care, and wardrobe. I was not a fashionista. My pop-bottle eyeglasses covered half my face (a tragic 1980s fashion trend). A mouth full of braces completed a look that could kill. If I ever forgot that, I was often reminded by some snarky seventh-grade girl. Or, much worse, by a boy who took stock of my assets and found serious deficits. I desperately needed all the help L'Oreal, Vidal Sassoon, and Gloria Vanderbilt could deliver. In high school, the glasses gave way to contacts and the braces to a beautiful smile. I learned how to be an "Easy, Breezy Cover Girl." But the deep wounds of those years remained.

When my daughter, Molly, reached that age, I envisioned my adolescent apocalypse repeating itself. Before she started middle school, I took her to my beauty salon for a stylish haircut. When she wanted to wear makeup in sixth grade, I made a beeline to the drugstore. Her wardrobe was the envy of her friends. By golly, I was going to give her what my mother did not.

Over time, I realized my behavior was really about me and my wounds. I believed if she felt pretty, confidence would follow. I found out that it's not that simple. And an overemphasis on appearance was not in her best interest.

Ways Our Relationship With Our Moms Can Affect Us

Confidence level. How confident we feel about being a mother is often partly a reflection of how well-equipped we are. How relaxed and confident were our own mothers?

Kathy

My mothering apprenticeship started early with the birth of my sister's baby when I was just thirteen. My mother taught me everything I needed to know about caring for babies. You name it—swaddling, rocking, feeding—I had it down. I had stored up lots of knowledge by the time I had to take the test. However, all of this experience didn't translate into complete mothering bliss.

Melinda

Personally, I brought my mother's anxiety into my mothering. I never felt relaxed. And I didn't feel like I could go to my mother as a resource for advice. For many years, I felt too much shame to reach out to others.

Effectiveness. Nicole is a homeschooling mom who also runs a business from her home. It's a combination that's working beautifully for her family. And she credits the example her mother set for her as the key to her success. "My mom was very intentional about expressing the value of motherhood. She ran a business from home, too, and showed me how that could blend well with family life," she explains. "I'm so glad that she asked me questions like, 'How is your career going to affect your role as a wife and mother someday?' This approach is very countercultural, but my kids are reaping the benefits of placing a high priority on motherhood and family life."

Amy had a very different, tragic experience with her mother. Her parents divorced when she was seven years old. A couple years later, Amy's mom decided that motherhood was becoming a barrier to her new life of men and heavy drug use. Throughout her adolescence, Amy's mother was completely absent. Now she feels ill-prepared and ineffective as she's raising her girls. "How am I ever going to teach my girls to feel good about themselves—their sexuality, their womanhood—when my mother was never around to teach me these things so I could learn from her?" she says. "Mothers are supposed to be the backbone of the family. Mine was never there, so I came into motherhood feeling very unstable. I've had to compensate for this by going to counseling, asking for advice from trusted sources, and taking parenting classes."

 Lovin' Spoonful

The loving example of motherhood that a mother gives to her daughter will empower generations to come. Let that truth motivate and propel your mothering.

Mothering style. In most cases, it's not a "take it or leave it" process as we develop our mothering style. As we grow as mothers and in our walk with God, we expand on some methods and allow Him to filter out others that aren't working.

"I had a great mom, just not a godly mom," says Donna, mom of two adult children. "She was strict, tough, and independent. She made me strong, and I definitely took some of that approach into my mothering. I was a strict, hard mom." But in her midtwenties, Donna became a Christian, and her whole view of motherhood changed. "My mom taught me how to love my kids with emotions. Through Jesus, I learned how to love them with my life. I began to practice sacrificial love with my children. I worked hard to be consistent in my parenting. But I also brought in grace. I'm more mushy than my mom was. It's important to go there [examining our relationship with our moms], we just can't stay there. We have to focus on moving forward."

> In most cases, it's not a "take it or leave it" process as we develop our mothering style.

Religious formation. Parents have a pivotal role in our view of God and how we approach the spiritual. This is something we need to keep in the forefront of our minds as we're mothering our own children. The passing on of faith can be messy. There are no guarantees. We want to be deliberate, but at the same time avoid presenting only rules without relationship.

Nicole, the homeschooling mom we discussed earlier, was fortunate to have a mother who modeled an active and vibrant relationship with God. "Although we went to church every Sunday, it was watching my mom and dad live out their faith that really impacted me. It affected every aspect of our lives," she says. "My mom wasn't afraid of my questions about faith. She allowed me to search for truth by encouraging me to read and placing good, solid resources into my hands."

Forgiving and Letting Go of the Past

We've seen that our mothers have influenced us in both positive and negative ways. So what do we do with the bad stuff? How do we resolve the anger, disappointment, or resentment we may have for the ways our mothers hurt us? The areas they didn't equip us? The times they failed us?

Whatever our stories may be, our children deserve healing mothers. Notice we didn't say *healed*. It's a process, one that takes years of God's grace and mercy. Regardless of whether our mothers, fathers, or other relatives didn't exactly prepare us for parenthood, our children didn't ask for wounded mothers. They just need our love. In Charles Stanley's book, *Landmines in the Path of the Believer*, he says this about forgiveness:

> We are to forgive so that we may enjoy God's goodness without feeling the weight of anger burning deep within our hearts. Forgiveness does not mean we recant the fact that what happened to us was wrong. Instead, we roll our burdens onto the Lord and allow Him to carry them for us.[2]

God is willing and able. In Matthew 11:29–30, Jesus tells us, "Take my yoke upon you and learn from me, for I am gentle and humble in heart, and you will find rest for your souls. For my yoke is easy and my burden is light." Exercising our faith enables us to move beyond the wounds of the past and allows us to draw on God's power as we heal.

> Whatever our stories may be, our children deserve healing mothers. Notice we didn't say **healed**.

Forgiveness is not a one-time event. We have to nurture this spirit of forgiveness throughout our mothering lives. Amy, who was abandoned by her mother at age nine, says it this way: "It took me years to process my pain. I can't have a relationship with my mom, but I'm able to forgive my mom. How? Because Jesus is walking beside me the whole time. When I turn my anger and resentment over to Him, He empowers me to forgive her. I'm not alone. He will never abandon me."

First, we think it's important to understand what forgiveness is and *isn't*. In Suzie Eller's book *The Unburdened Heart*, she describes it this way:

> Forgiveness is an intentional act to let go of the burden and restrictions of bitterness, anger, rage or unresolved emotions connected to a person or event. In other words, forgiveness is surrender. It's offering up resentment. It's giving up the desire to punish. It's letting go of anger. It's getting out of the "debt collection" business.[3]

How do we get to that place? Here are a few practical ways to move toward forgiveness:

Pray, pray, and pray some more. It's the key. And not just a prayer that says, "Help me." A true prayer of empowerment admits our complete inability to forgive on our own. It asks God to give us His forgiveness. In her book *The Hiding Place*, Corrie ten Boom tells a story of when she once crossed paths with a man who had committed grave wrongs against her and her sister:

> I breathed a silent prayer. *Jesus, I cannot forgive him. Give Your forgiveness.* As I took his hand the most incredible thing happened. . . . Into my heart sprang a love for this stranger that almost overwhelmed me. And so I discovered that it is not on our forgiveness any more than on our goodness that the world's healing hinges, but on His.[4]

Ask questions. Either of your mom or of other relatives. Our perception of past wounds may be off track.

Kathy

My mom never encouraged us to have friends sleep over or have company for dinner. I thought she was being mean. I found out later that it was mostly due to financial reasons. As a struggling single mom, she simply couldn't afford to feed one more mouth one more meal.

Quit expecting what they're not giving. Every unmet expectation is another inflicted wound. It builds resentment and hinders the forgiveness and moving-on process.

Melinda

The more I understood about my mother's mental illness and her inability to treat it properly, the more I realized that she was simply unable to give me the level of emotional support and feedback I craved. I quit expecting it. She couldn't give that. Period. That realization helped me to move on. Expecting what we know our mothers can't or won't give is not productive and can keep us in a place of chronic disappointment. Again, we can't do this alone. Making this shift in our expectations has to be empowered by our faith walk and dependence on Jesus.

Seek professional, godly counseling. Both of us have done this and found it has helped us move past areas of paralysis and resentment.

Develop empathy. Sometimes it can help to view our upbringing from our moms' perspective.

Melinda

Even after my mom died of cancer, I still held some latent resentment about the things I felt she couldn't give me that I needed. Then my kids got older. Molly hit middle school. Micah was nearing the preteen years. Mothering suddenly got a whole lot harder. I gained a lot more compassion and empathy for my mom and her struggles. She was doing the most she was capable of doing. When I started seeing it in that light, I was able to give her so much more grace.

Focus on the positive things given to us by our mothers. Lizbeth had a tragic upbringing with a paranoid and abusive mother. "She introduced me to a very warped kind of faith in God. But I'm still so grateful that she introduced me to Him," she says.

Lovin' Spoonful

A Prayer of Forgiveness

Lord, I lift up my mom. Help her to draw close to You and to know Your love for her. Grant me eyes to recognize the gifts she gave me. Empower me to forgive those things she's done that hurt me. Please forgive me for being unforgiving. Forgive me for holding on to what You let go of on the cross. Help me to find peace through You and to extend that peace toward my mother. Amen.

"Through the Holy Spirit, I absorbed some important truths about God, regardless of how they were presented. Later, I had to filter out a lot of the lies, but my faith journey started with my mother."

We all must find a way to move forward in our own mothering journeys. Good or bad, we're not our mothers. Our ultimate goal has to be to recognize the positive things they handed to us and forgive the wounds. This process will empower our mothering.

I look back on the lack of grace I showed my mom during difficult times and am ashamed of myself. . . . It's never too late to show her that grace.

—Emily, mother of two

Stirring Your Thoughts

1. Write five words to describe the relationship you had or have with your mom.
2. What are three positive things about your mother?

3. What are a few habits or tendencies you learned or inherited from your mom?
   - Which do you want to continue and pass down?
   - Which do you want to leave in the past?
4. As you think about your mother, ask yourself this: In what areas do *you* want to be given grace by *your* children as they think back on you as a mother someday?
5. What did your mother teach you about God?
6. What is the one place you need to start forgiving your mother today? Remember, it's a process, not an event.

Let's Get Cookin'

- Don't put off a conversation with your mother expressing your gratitude for all of the positive things she gave you. The example you set in this area will not go unnoticed by your children.

- Looking back, have you realized your mom was acting in your best interest, even though you were upset and angry with her at the time? Tell her. Thank her for being your advocate even when it meant risking your wrath or being misunderstood.

- If your mother is unavailable (either through death or circumstance), writing a letter and getting all of your feelings, thoughts, and questions on paper can be very cathartic and enlightening. Read it out loud—either alone or with a trusted friend—to help process any emotional response.

Chapter 8

Tasting and Seeing
What Is Good

When we first became mothers over twenty years ago, finding mothering resources was not as convenient as sitting at a keyboard or picking up our smart phones. We made trips to the bookstore. Mommy connections were randomly made at schools, churches, or Mommy and Me classes. If we were lucky, we discussed our problems with a trusted few: mom, sisters, and a couple close friends. Now we have the entire world to consult when making a choice. Overnight, it seemed, every question we had could be Googled. An onslaught of mom blogs, online forums, and social media has largely replaced regular, one-on-one, face-to-face conversations.

Clearly, in the Information Age, limitless choices can be overwhelming. How do we know which advice will be wise and fruitful for our families? Developing boundaries and discernment is crucial to creating our own recipe for mothering. This comes more naturally for some of us than others. However, it's a valuable skill that we all can learn.

Being self-disciplined as we interact with all the information available is always in our best interest, as well as our children's. None of us can afford to be impulsive and random as we take in advice that influences the mothering of our precious children. Rather, if we make God-driven, deliberate choices, we'll be empowered to move forward and mother with confidence.

Cleansing Our Palate

We're called to "test everything; hold fast what is good" (1 Thessalonians 5:21 ESV)—that includes the mothering advice, resources, and support we seek and implement.

Melinda

For example, shortly after Molly's birth, I began having some health problems. I realized my typical American junk-food diet wasn't helping. I decided to embark on a radical eating makeover. I went from mindlessly giving in to my cravings and eating whatever sounded good, to being careful and discriminating about what I chose to put into my mouth. Before, my taste buds were so desensitized, I didn't even recognize good nourishment. However, soon the things I used to eat didn't even appeal to me. The same principle can be applied as we select and consume nourishment for our mothering souls.

 Lovin' Spoonful

Taste Testing Test

When deciding whether to heed a piece of advice, ask yourself the following questions (based on Philippians 4:8):

Is it true?
Is it noble?
Is it right?
Is it pure?
Is it lovely?

We need to be discerning consumers, if you will, when it comes to whom and what we let influence and teach us. It's important to create boundaries and limits to our exposure. We can easily become overwhelmed and paralyzed. What does God have to say about true wisdom? Proverbs 2 tells us to turn our "ear to wisdom" and apply our "heart to understanding." Later, it says "look for it as for silver and search for it as for hidden treasure, then you will understand the fear of the Lord and find the knowledge of God" (vv. 2, 4–5). Seeking true wisdom is clearly not easy. It's hidden and valuable. This isn't a passive exercise, where we just absorb everything that's thrown at us.

> Developing boundaries and discernment is crucial to creating our own recipe for motherhood.

Chasing after attention, validation, and stimulation is much more tempting. In the current age, social media is the always-accessible provider for all of those needs. It can literally become a substitute for a relationship with God. There is no accountability and soul-searching with the Internet. No requirements are placed upon us. Our fleshly nature controls the interaction, and that's never a good idea. Our Creator calls us to real relationship through rising to a high standard of unconditional love and continual self-examination, gently guided by His Holy Spirit. This is definitely harder, more challenging, and more uncomfortable than worshiping at the feet of the social media god. But the true God provides lasting satisfaction, not a fleeting feeling.

Here are a few guidelines we've found helpful to sort through all the noise and information we have access to as we mother our children:

Be prayerful. Let's be deliberate about taking the Holy Spirit to our computers. We need to pray often and specifically about what we take in via our computer screens. Every sin we ever commit, every distortion of the enemy we accept as truth, begins in the mind. Every. Single. One. So doesn't it make sense for us to ruthlessly filter what we put into it? Here's a verse that may be helpful for us

Lovin' Spoonful

We aren't going to always make the right choices, even with our best intentions.

Remember, "all things work together for good" (Romans 8:28 ESV).

to keep on an index card by our computers: "Do not conform to the pattern of this world, but be transformed by the renewing of your mind. Then you will be able to test and approve what God's will is—his good, pleasing and perfect will" (Romans 12:2). This applies when seeking and filtering face-to-face information, as well.

Be courageous. This means cutting out negative influences—either online or in real life—or anything else that doesn't support our roles as moms in a positive way. Disconnect from or delete social media conversations that aren't productive. We've both found the need to block people who aren't encouraging positive thoughts or feelings. This means people who tear down motherhood or those who inspire feelings of jealousy and inadequacy in us.

Be a good steward. Online mom forums and websites have opened up a great well of support for mothers. But it's possible to consume too much of a good thing. Once again, the Holy Spirit has to remain our main guide. Further, we can spend so much time talking *about* our children online that we never actually talk *to* our children. Set boundaries in the form of time limits and times of day to be online. Let's choose those times when our children are otherwise occupied. We need to be present—physically and mentally—when they are.

Be accountable. Once we've created boundaries, we're wise to ask others to help keep us on track. It can be as simple as asking our husbands, "Do you think I've been online too much lately?" Or we can check in with a friend, even on Facebook, on a weekly basis for feedback about our social media interaction. We're constantly asking each other about how to respond to sometimes sticky dialogue online.

Be cautious of seeking out "echoes." It can be tempting to listen to only those sources that agree with us. Cherry-picking information and opinions is not seeking true wisdom. Going to primarily those sources we know will validate our mind-set or the decisions we've already made can be dangerous if our thinking is misguided.

> We can spend so much time talking **about** our children online that we never actually talk **to** our children.

Who Do We Let In?

Jesus is the first Person we should invite into our mothering. He's the Guest of Honor, the gold standard against which we measure all other counsel. Spending regular time in His Word and prayer is the best way to know His standard and ways intimately enough to use them as our measuring stick. In chapter 13, we'll be giving valuable, practical tips for incorporating time with Jesus into our mommy routines, no matter how crazy.

Although we shouldn't place an exaggerated amount of faith in human advice, the Bible clearly tells us the value of seeking godly counsel. But what does that look like? If we don't know, we can easily get burned. We have both been there a few times. Through painful trial and error and by looking to the Bible for direction, we've found some key characteristics that godly people possess:

They're spirited. We can spot them by their fruit. According to Galatians 5:22–23, that means we can look at their lives and see ample evidence of "love, joy, peace, patience, kindness, goodness, faithfulness, gentleness and self-control" (NLT). Sometimes in a jaded world it can be hard to find "fruitful" people. We have the benefit of this beautiful Scripture to help us identify godly action in their lives.

They're humble. Godly people are willing to shatter their image for our benefit. If they've made mistakes or had experiences that are relevant to our situation, they share them with us freely. They live out the truth of Romans 12:3: "Do not think of yourself more highly than you ought, but rather think of yourself with sober judgment, in accordance with the faith God has distributed to each of you."

> Godly people are willing to shatter their image for our benefit.

They're merciful, not judgmental. Just like Jesus when faced with the adulterous woman in John 8, they speak honestly, but they don't throw stones. These are the folks that can see us for our "warts and all" and still love us.

They're trustworthy. Nothing we say is disclosed inappropriately. That's why we feel encouraged to seek them for advice for our most personal issues.

They're honest. They're not afraid to speak truth to our situation even if it's hard to hear. In Ephesians 4:15, Paul tells us that mature believers are "speaking the truth in love."

They're credible. They've been walking with Jesus long enough to have a deep knowledge of Him and His counsel and faithfulness. Their words and advice match up with their actions. James 2:18 sums it up well: "Show me your faith without deeds, and I will show you my faith by my deeds."

They're wise with their words. Offering guidance is a huge responsibility. Godly people don't give out recommendations lightly. And they admit when they're wrong. "Do you see someone who speaks in haste? There is more hope for a fool than for them" (Proverbs 29:20).

In some circumstances, we may need to seek out godly, professional counselors. Some examples might include significant behavior issues with kids, marital difficulties, or problems with extended family. Again, this is where courageousness comes in.

For both of us, counseling has been a strong component to becoming healthier moms. These professionals have seen it all. Our concerns aren't new to them. What takes the most courage is to take that very first step of a phone call.

Kathy

During the time that I was the most depressed, Christian counselors served as the objective voice of reason I needed to hear. They helped make sense of my scattered mind.

Following Our God-Given Gut

Seeking godly counsel, especially as we face complicated or difficult struggles, is both beneficial and biblical. But always keep in mind that human advice and perceptions can be flawed, even when they're offered with the best intentions. So why are we often more quick to listen to those voices than we are to the Counselor that God has given us in the form of His Holy Spirit—the only Counselor who will never steer us wrong?

The problem can be that our minds are never quiet enough to hear that voice. Worries, fears, the Internet and other media, and the crazy pace of family life can all but drown out the subtle promptings—a nudge, a thought—that the Holy Spirit is giving us. We're so busy or distracted that we dismiss the uneasiness in our gut that signals that we should exercise caution or pay closer attention.

As moms, we can be uncomfortable with silence. It's foreign to us! We have to make a conscious choice to periodically pull away from the chaos. Jesus is our example. He did it regularly in order to stay in tune with the Father, and He was the Son of God! How can we think we mere mortal mamas don't need to do it? Even if we can't get away physically, we can train our minds to escape from the noise. What does this look like? Well, it can take a lot of different forms: an Internet fast; getting up even a few minutes before the rest of the family to sit in a quiet house, read His Word, and

Lovin' Spoonful

I believe in your commands; now teach me good judgment and knowledge.

Psalm 119:66 (NLT)

pray in the silence; or turning off the radio in the parent pickup line and just being still.

Sometimes we can purposely avoid the silence. We know what the Holy Spirit would say to our circumstance—and frankly we don't want to hear it. His counsel is rarely the easy way, and it often pushes us out of our comfort zone. This avoidance often takes two forms:

Rationalizing. Let's call it what it really is, shall we? It's a compromise of our core values. But it doesn't seem like it.

Kathy

A number of years ago, I discovered one of our children was playing video games in excess of three to four hours on any given day. It was something I didn't want to know. It was easier for me to say, "Hey, he's a great kid. He makes good grades, goes to church, and is sweet to his family." However, it still compromised a core family value I thought I was teaching: making good use of time. If I was going to be serious and intentional about supporting that value, I had to call a spade a spade.

Overthinking.

Melinda

I'm the reigning Queen of Overthinking. Here's what it looks like: I know that the Holy Spirit is leading me to handle an issue or problem with one of my children in a way that makes me squirm. But instead of acting, I analyze and debate all the pros and cons over and over again in my head. I imagine all the potential pitfalls. It's an exercise that's rooted in fear. And it keeps me frozen in inaction. In the meantime, the issue doesn't go away. In fact, it usually gets worse. But I remain in perpetual inner turmoil. And my children are truly the ones who suffer.

Here's some of the inner dialogue that goes on inside my twisted little mind: *Am I being too harsh? What if I'm wrong? Maybe I'm overreacting. Is this going to damage my relationship with him or her? What if he or she reacts badly and pulls away from me? What if this causes them to rebel?*

So what cuts through the confusion, the overthinking, the rationalizing? Obedience. We know what to do through His Word and through prayer. He's not the God of confusion (1 Corinthians 14:33). When we obey what we know in our gut that God is telling us, things become simple. By simple, we don't mean easy. But the path that we should take becomes clear as we begin to step out in obedience.

Our families are always the beneficiaries when we're perceptive and discerning. When we ask God to "create in [us] a clean heart" (Psalm 51:10 esv), then we permit Him to move freely in guiding us toward discernment and wisdom.

> I was going to write a [blog] post about my son a few months ago, and the instant I started I knew I shouldn't. . . . It is not something I would love for him to read in the future, so I just deleted it and wrote something else.
>
> —Tia, mother of three

Stirring Your Thoughts

1. Psalm 34:8 says, "Taste and see that the Lord is good; blessed is the one who takes refuge in him." What does it mean to you to "taste and see" God's goodness?

2. What are some of the resources you go to most frequently for advice?

3. On a scale from 1 to 5 (5 being very godly), how godly are these resources?

4. How confident are you in your ability to make wise decisions?

5. Where is one place you find yourself rationalizing (making something okay when it's not or ignoring something important) in your mothering?

6. In what areas of your mothering do you tend to get paralyzed by overthinking?

Let's Get Cookin'

• Seek out three new resources that uphold your family's values.

• Perform a social media purge. Go through each of your profiles, each friend, connection, and newsfeed. Are they negative? Do they support your values? When you read something from that particular source (whether it's an organization, group, or individual), does it make you feel inadequate, jealous, less-than, angry, resentful, or just plain lousy? Remove the exposure. It's okay.

• Look at your answers to numbers 5 and 6 in "Stirring Your Thoughts." Pick one place that you perpetually rationalize or overthink in your mothering. Ask one friend to hold you accountable to making a change in these patterns.

The Online World: What's a Mom to Do?

Many healthy and encouraging mom connections can be made online. In fact, we're both better for the wisdom and friendships we've developed with some amazing mamas. Still, we have to ac-knowledge the dark temptation and tantalizing force associated with the online mommy experience. Misery loves company—and lots of it. Venting about the trials and annoyances of motherhood is not new. Women have been doing it for centuries, but the conversations remained between two close friends. Those gripes were "between you, me, and the fence post." When mothers vent now, it's between you, me, and all of cyberspace. And if our children aren't old enough to read now, they will be someday.

It's in our fleshly nature to complain. We've been doing this since the dawn of man. Adam and Eve just had each other. She hadn't made 522 Facebook friends who could follow her every struggle with little Cain and Abel's nasty habit of sibling rivalry. The seemingly harmless post about your child's annoying habit can bring tons of comments and public commiseration, but it has the potential to inflict plenty of harm when the child stumbles upon it. This takes place in text and Facebook messages, not just blogs. Just imagine that every post we write, every text we send, and every Facebook status we post was placed in a time capsule. And we have to give it to our children when they turn sixteen. That should sober us up quick.

Our venting can affect our children and families in other ways, as well, even if they never see our rantings. Because while "what happens in Vegas, stays in Vegas" (not really), our negativ-ity grows virally. The more we rant and rave and it's validated, the more we project that pessimism and resentment into our relationships with our children. Sometimes we tend to think that if something is true, it's okay to type it. But just because it's true doesn't mean it's productive or loving. Not every childhood event or moment should be photographed and shared. Let's treat our kids with the same respect and dignity that we would want.

Here are a few important questions to ask yourself before serving it up online:

1. Does this glorify God, or me? "And whatever you do, whether in word or deed, do it all in the name of the Lord Jesus, giving thanks to God the Father through him" (Colossians 3:17).

2. Does this hurt anyone or cause my brother (or sister) to stumble? "Be careful, however, that the exercise of your rights does not become a stumbling block to the weak" (1 Corinthians 8:9).

3. If this were plastered on a billboard in the middle of my hometown, would I still be okay with it? "For whatever is hidden is meant to be disclosed, and whatever is concealed is meant to be brought out into the open" (Mark 4:22). One of the fruits of the Spirit is self-control.

4. What are the possible repercussions from saying or not saying something? How will it affect others—most importantly my family?

5. Does this reflect Jesus? Would He "Like" it or "Share" it?

6. Is it productive? Or is it exhibitionism vs. confession?

Chapter 9
Mom Mentors: Turning Rivals to Resources

We'd like to invite you on a journey that will enrich your mothering in amazing and unexpected ways. Just like parenting, this trip won't always be smooth, but it can be supremely satisfying. Are you in? We're talking about the search for helpful mothering guides, or mentors. But where do we find them? That's a good and very tricky question. You'll probably pursue some relationships that don't work out. But those that do can make all the difference.

Mothers shouldn't be wandering alone in the wilderness. We require encouragement and support from strong role models and reliable resources. Even if society and the voice of the enemy say you're better off on your own, it's simply not true. A solo journey is not what God intended. Proverbs 27:17 tells us, "As iron sharpens iron, so one person sharpens another."

Often we don't seek connection because we're "getting by" just fine on our own. Our sense of pride and fear of vulnerability or appearing inadequate are often the barrier to our own happiness. Whatever the reason, we've decided that mere survival is enough. This is the essence of the lie we've come to believe. But God has

Lovin' Spoonful

Our confidence will falter in isolation. Our thinking processes are a battleground between lie and fact. Reaching out to others enables the Holy Spirit to work through community, helping to fight the lies of the enemy. Unless we're constantly sustained by biblical truth, our thoughts turn toward guilt and inadequacy. We need to lean on the strength and discernment of the Holy Spirit to sift through those temporary feelings and embrace reality.

designed us for community. Isolation is fertile ground for Satan to take hold of our minds and hearts.

In Titus 2, Paul outlines the importance of older women teaching younger women how to be godly women, wives, and mothers. Over the years, we both struggled to find mom mentors—those moms who can provide support and guidance. We searched for them. We prayed for them. We even directly begged for their help. The Titus 2 woman we longed for never made an appearance. It's not her fault. Our present culture doesn't encourage sharing the time and being available for a traditional one-on-one mentoring relationship.

Commonly, we think of the Titus 2 model as an older woman. But we've discovered that someone's depth of experience in certain areas can far exceed her age in years. Twenty-something or thirty-something moms may seem naïve and youthful, but we don't know their stories and what they're able to contribute to our lives. Also, sometimes it's helpful to have someone sharing wisdom who is still "in the trenches" or has very recently been there. She can possess a more direct, more easily accessible empathy than someone who hasn't been in that situation for a number of years. This type of mom mentor is someone we call "relationally appropriate," not necessarily someone who has more years on you and therefore someone you think has more to offer. We need to reframe our thinking on exactly what a wisdom-giving mom can look like.

We discovered that we are well served by gaining support and guidance from multiple sources. Women who are our peers can also be our mentors in one or more areas of our mothering. We refer to this as a "Moms Together" approach.

We are in this together and can draw and learn from one another's wisdom and experience. "Moms Together" is a mind-set. It's a willingness to look for moms who are more skilled, knowledgeable, or experienced than we are in a specific area of mothering—those who share that wisdom freely, lovingly, and sometimes unknowingly.

We found this type of relationship in each other. Neither of us had a gray hair on our head (nor will we ever, thanks to our local salon). We were both in our thirties. We didn't possess the wisdom of Solomon. And we so desperately needed it. However, even though we were close to the same age, we *did* have different experiences and strengths from which the other could benefit. Who knew? We didn't at first.

Women who are our peers can also be our mentors in one or more areas of our mothering.

Kathy

For example, I was a rebellious kid. I was too big for my britches. I was physically mature beyond my years, but my psyche had some catching up to do. I was a handful. My teenage years were full of academic and relational struggles. As I watched Melinda wrestle with her then-tween daughter's strong-willed personality, I could relate in a way she could not.

Melinda

The most rebellious thing I did as a teenager was get my ears double-pierced. Crazy times, huh? So I had no idea what to do with my "handful" tween. But Kathy could explain to me how her mind worked and gave me some ideas that I would've never thought of on my own. She understood Molly because she had *been* Molly. Plus, it was just comforting to know that rebellious young Kathy survived and ultimately thrived. And so did Kathy's mother.

At first, our relationship developed mostly informally through phone calls as we waited in the parent pickup line. Slowly, we began to share more of ourselves, our struggles, and our fears. This didn't happen overnight. It was a gradual but steady process, as our trust and comfort levels grew. If either of us had sensed we were being judged or evaluated, our relationship would've never taken off. Personally, I was in a difficult place where I needed advice and feedback about struggles with my children. It couldn't be about me, my pride, or my image. I knew I needed this kind of honest relationship to grow my character and my mothering because it was necessary for the health of my family.

Kathy

I had just had a bad experience with a supposedly close friend. The experience left me shell-shocked and closed off. What kept me continuing the relationship with Melinda was her openness. I didn't feel like I was always the vulnerable one.

With each pickup-line chat, colorful text conversation, and ballpark bleacher heart-to-heart, we gradually realized we were giving valuable feedback that was helping meet each other's mentoring need. Our connection piqued our awareness of the resources that we could be to each other as mothers, even though we were the same age. We also realized the wealth of knowledge we provided to each other because of the range of ages and genders of our six children. We can't discount the wisdom we can gain from mothers who have children who are just a few years older than ours.

If only we had known that wisdom isn't exclusive to little gray-haired ladies, it would've saved us a lot of misery. We knew of each other for years, as we crossed paths in the hallways of Ben's (Kathy's husband) pediatric office. But it was when we were sitting on bleachers together day after day while our children played on the same baseball team that we began to invest in each other. We had a lot more to share than just sunscreen.

Unsolicited and Solicited Guidance

How do we find these mentors? Do we wait until one of these wise moms crosses our path? The "Moms Together" attitude can commonly manifest itself in two ways: unsolicited and solicited guidance. Unsolicited mom mentors are like God's grace. They just show up! A "random act of mothering kindness" is a great example of this kind of help.

Melinda

As a first-time mommy, I was struggling with breastfeeding. It didn't come easily and I didn't like it. This was my first taste of the deadly combo of mothering guilt and inadequacy. My mother wasn't close-by or accessible. I was sore, emotional, and completely overwhelmed.

My then-pastor's wife (who ended up becoming a close friend) showed up at my door unannounced and armed with a new-mommy care package. It was loaded with Aquaphor, breast pads, and some breastfeeding resources. She didn't know how much I was struggling, but she was a more experienced mom who could imagine what I was going through, and followed her impulse to reach out to me.

An appropriate response to this type of outreach can actually encourage more of it and help us develop deeper, supportive relationships. It doesn't need to be an elaborate thank-you gesture. In this day and age, a text or Facebook message can suffice. Perhaps think of a small way you can repay the kindness that would meet a need of theirs. Or even pay it forward and think about who you can bless in a similar way. Who else needs the kindness and mom help

Lovin' Spoonful

A Mentoring Prayer for Moms

Dear Father,

Thank You for the gift of my children.

My desire is to raise them according to Your will and standards. I cannot do this alone. Please give me the power of Your Holy Spirit, as well as a teachable heart.

Help me to recognize women who cross my path who can strengthen and encourage me in the vocation You have given me.

Keep my heart open to unlikely sources of inspiration and guidance.

Help me also to see the need in other mothers and be willing to reach out as You direct. Amen.

that you've been offered? It doesn't take long to look outside our four walls and find someone who could benefit from our outreach.

Unsolicited guidance can also come in the form of observing someone doing something worth emulating. We can make a practical application of what we've observed them doing in our own mothering.

When Sherri was a young college student, her family had a friend, a single mom whom her parents mentored for years. "Our family spent tons of time with her. I always noticed that every time her kids acted up, she would lean over and whisper something in their ears. They would instantly shape up and start behaving," says Sherri. "I knew then, even at my young age, that I would discipline my children the same way. I had seen my friends' parents yell at them, belittle them, or talk over them. And I observed the frustration that caused. I was determined not to do that to my own children. So when my kids hit their toddler years, I employed her discipline technique, particularly out in public. When they would act out, I would lean over and whisper in their ears, 'That behavior is not appropriate. I want you to stop.' Or, 'Your choices are making others uncomfortable. Do you need to take a break to calm down?' The technique worked wonders on my kids and I never really had any of those awkward public moments when you yell at your kids and lots of people turn and stare, and all involved are uncomfortable and unsettled.

"Years later, I saw this friend again on one of her trips through town. We were catching up on our lives and kids. I decided to tell her how she had influenced my parenting long before parenting was ever on my radar. It occurred to me during our visit that I never knew what she had said to her own kids when she leaned over to whisper in their ears. So I asked her about it.

"She told me she said the same thing every time: 'You're embarrassing me. Would you like me to embarrass you?'"

Like Sherri, we can take the parenting methods we observe in other mothers and make them our own so that they fit our personalities and our children's. These kinds of discoveries are made "on the fly." They're little mothering gifts from heaven. We can ask God to help us recognize them.

Actually soliciting wise advice requires a little more effort and planning on our part. But it's not impossible. We promise. Here are a few ways we can make it happen:

Open our hearts. Are our hearts teachable? Are we willing to put our pride aside and learn from others? If not, we need to pray and ask for the Holy Spirit's help; it's not something we can do on our own. But let's do it before we reach a point of painful desperation.

Kathy

I'm an English teacher by trade. My degree is in education. I used to have a tutoring business for kids with special needs when my husband was in residency. Imagine my surprise when, as a mother, some of my own children didn't respond to my miraculous teaching techniques. They needed a different kind of help. I started asking mothers of older, successful students for names of tutors. I targeted mothers with children who had overcome significant academic challenges. I ended up finding an unlikely hero for me (because I was woefully ineffective) and for my kids. He was a burly baseball coach who spoke fluent high school-ese. And he happened to have a PhD in English.

I learned a valuable lesson about finding mothering assistance. He wasn't a mom, yet he reached my own children in a way I couldn't. And I learned from watching his example and realized I could apply his motivation and teaching techniques to other areas of my mothering.

Open our eyes. Let's say we observe a mom who always seems to be on time to church. She doesn't appear to have gone three rounds in a boxing ring before entering the sanctuary. We, on the other hand, seem to be screeching into the parking lot fifteen minutes late with a car full of stressed-out kids. Maybe there's something we can learn from her. She would be flattered if we asked her secret. The only thing it requires is a little courage and humility.

Open our doors. Small gestures of hospitality go a long way. We have to get over our lived-in houses and invite people into our messy lives. It's an instant way to connect and go to a deeper level with others.

Open our mouths. Compliment that mom who gets her kids to church on time. It breaks the ice, and who doesn't like a little flattery? Then ask her for help or advice. We can do this anywhere and at any time.

Turning Rivals to Resources

Peer-to-peer mentoring requires a change of perspective. We have to quit viewing each other through the lens of competition. We aren't rivals. We can be resources instead. Making the shift in our minds, viewing other mothers as valuable resources, will set us free in so many ways:

Free from condemnation.

Free from the need to measure up.

Free from going it alone.

In Romans 8:1, Paul tells us, "Therefore, there is now no condemnation for those who are in Christ Jesus."

> Why not take mothering out of the category of competition?

As we shared before, what we're really talking about is forming a teachable heart—one that's open and willing to explore and make sometimes uncomfortable and inconvenient choices. It's ultimately for our own good and the benefit of our children. We encounter plenty of competition in our lives, especially concerning our kids. Why not take mothering out of the category of competition?

Sometimes it may require us to relinquish a little bit of power and control in our children's lives. *Ouch.* That hurts just thinking about it, doesn't it? But it's not all about us. If the goal is to do what's best for our children, then we have to be willing to get out of the way. At times, that's what the situation requires.

Melinda

As I mentioned earlier, the middle school years with my daughter placed me in uncharted territory. I felt like I was constantly being yanked from my comfort zone and left gasping for air. Somewhere in the middle of this time, my daughter began to form a connection with a young mom at our church. She was bubbly and hip but godly and wise beyond her years. I would watch her interact and connect with Molly in a way I simply could not. I reached out to this mom and asked her to make a point of regularly interacting with my daughter. She loved Molly and was all too willing. I also asked her advice about how I could better connect with and understand Molly. Her involvement and insights made a huge difference in both Molly's life and mine.

Years later, this mom told me she still prays for Molly regularly. And it all started with a simple request.

Safety First in Finding Mom Mentors

As moms, we're continually concerned with our children's influences and safety. But we also need to be concerned about our own potential experiences when we're looking for mom mentors. Selecting them requires divine discernment. We've both been burned by unsafe people who either took advantage of our vulnerability or misrepresented themselves and their motives.

We've both taken women into our confidence, even though our gut was screaming, "Beware!" This is where our mothering instinct kicks in, and we need to follow it as we pray for God to bring the right people into our lives.

Melinda

I remember having thoughts like, *She's a Christian. Everyone else seems to like her. I must be off base.* But in each instance, the signals my gut was sending were spot on. At that point, I would often take a "don't offer, don't refuse" approach to the relationship. I wouldn't initiate contact or conversations with the person in question, but I would still be cordial and polite when I saw her.

So what are some red flags that warn us of potentially unsafe advice-givers? They tend to be judgmental of others in our presence.

 Lovin' Spoonful

Passive-Aggressive: (adj.) being, marked by, or displaying behavior characterized by the expression of negative feelings, resentment, and aggression in an unassertive passive way (as through procrastination and stubbornness).[1]

A safe mom mentor is open, honest, and straightforward. Pray that God will help you be discerning as you search for them.

This is a clue that they might do the same to us when we're not around. Another red flag they wave is divulging personal information about others, sometimes under the guise of concern, but it's actually attention-seeking behavior, motivated by a need to appear "in the know." They can also exude an "I've got it all figured out" vibe. At first this can be attractive, but over time it results in a one-sided relationship—leaving us feeling like a "project" rather than a real friend.

Often, it's not so much *what* they say to us but *how* they say it. The tone is passive-aggressive, harsh (blunt), or subtly superior or demeaning. We feel like we're being talked down to.

Here are some things an unsafe advice-giver might say:

"I know that's not really your thing. Why don't you just let me do that?"

"Don't you need some help?"

"I'm so *blessed* not to have that problem!"

"Oh, we all did it. You'll survive."

What are some qualities of a safe mentor? They're open, approachable, and humble. There's no sense of a hidden agenda. There's no keeping score.

Here are some things you might hear a safe mentor say:

"I see you struggling. Can I share what worked for me?"

"Is there something I can do to be helpful?"

"I learned that one the hard way. Can I share my story with you?"

Kathy

You know that feeling when someone recognizes you struggling? I was drowning and my friend Nena just threw out life preserver after life preserver. She helped me in areas where I had always felt "less than" as a mother. Nena has the heavenly gift of order and organization. I don't. I didn't have anything heavenly going on in my house after my fourth child. Someone overheard me talking about my struggles and gave me her number in the middle of a soccer field.

I was just desperate enough to pick up the phone. Nena didn't preach. She just loved. Strange things spoke love to me during this time, like her teaching me how to straighten a pantry so I could find a stupid can of tomato soup. Her holy, organized hands lovingly guided me to so many "aha" moments. Who knew that unloading groceries could be a step-by-step task?

What is it for you, Mom? What does your heart need as you seek out those who can help in the areas where you struggle?

Excuses, Excuses: What Holds Us Back?

We've introduced you to the benefits of peer-to-peer mentoring as it applies to mothers. We now know the qualities of a good, safe mom mentor. Sometimes, however, an internal struggle can prevent us from reaching out. With God's help, we have to get past a few excuses that keep us isolated.

> We **all** need connection—regardless of our personality.

Excuse #1: "I'm not very outgoing." We *all* need connection—regardless of our personality. We can deny it or ignore it, but if we're honest with ourselves, we all have the desire to be understood.

At first it may feel a little forced, but we can all learn to become more comfortable with reaching out. Like anything, it requires practice. We all have something important and unique to offer. "Let your light shine before others, that they may see your good deeds and glorify your Father in heaven" (Matthew 5:16).

Excuse #2: "I'm not that interesting. No one really wants to spend time with me." To that, we say, why not let others be the judge of our charisma? We have no control over how someone feels about us; all we can do is say and do what we feel called to, follow the promptings of the Holy Spirit, and trust that He won't steer us wrong when it comes to who we're friends with. "For those who are led by the Spirit of God are the children of God. The Spirit you received does not make you slaves, so that you live in fear again" (Romans 8:14–15).

In Jill Savage's book *No More Perfect Moms*, she says,

> If reaching out to others is where fear stops you, take a first step by asking a mom to meet you somewhere away from home. Push through your fear of rejection and extend a hand of friendship. If she says no, ask someone else. Resist the urge to take that no answer personally; her schedule just might not allow the time for whatever activity you suggested.[2]

Excuse #3: "I'm so busy. I don't have time to connect." All of us are busy. We have to make plans, regardless of our schedules, or it won't happen. Do you want to get to know and learn from another mom? Then make it happen. And once you do, you'll experience the benefits: connection, valuable insights, understanding, and encouragement. And you'll want more. We suggest concentrating on reaching out to *one* person, rather than trying to create a whole tribe.

Melinda

Recently, I gave a mom that advice in an online forum. A few minutes later, I got this message from her: "I took your advice, Melinda. I focused on one person and asked her if she was busy tomorrow. We are getting together for a lunch play date! Looks like focusing on just one is the way to go!" This kind of small start can spark a relationship and builds courage. Further, it seems doable instead of overwhelming. So who is it that you need to connect with or who needs to connect with you? Perhaps God is calling you to be someone who attracts others to want to spend time with you!

Excuse #4: "I'm doing just fine by myself." Our response to this is to lovingly ask, "Is this denial on your part?" We need to do an

---

honest examination of what's at the root of our attitude. More likely, we're in shutdown mode. We may be overwhelmed and don't know where to start. Maybe we're just too tired to scale that mountain. (See the "Let's Get Cookin'" recommendation at end of chapter: Start small.) An island is simply not as fun to be on as an entire beach with plenty of women to talk with. Relationally, we aren't made for islands.

> Concentrate on reaching out to **one** person, rather than trying to create a whole tribe.

Excuse #5: "I've been burned when I've tried to connect with others in the past." It's no secret that most of us have been burned. Repeatedly. But what's the alternative? This is where we have to ask for the Holy Spirit's healing and His empowerment to forgive those who have wronged us. God can help us not only heal, but learn from those hurtful experiences. This process will help us bring more wisdom the next time we risk our hearts. It's hard to break out of past hurts, but we must or we'll never experience all that we're meant to experience in life. It's true for our relationships with our spouses and our children; surely it's true for our relationships with other women that God has designed us for.

Mothering *can* be sweet and satisfying. We *don't* have to do it alone. We *don't* have to live in a constant state of condemnation and inadequacy. Christ died to give us grace. He also gave us the gift of each other.

Sometimes our excuse is to put the blame on others: Nobody really "gets me," or "there are cliques." But even the Bible—in Proverbs—says that if you want to have friends, you should be one yourself! Sometimes we sit waiting for others to come and find us but we're not willing to get up and find others to connect with. It is hard but totally worth it!

—Michelle, mother of two

Stirring Your Thoughts

1. Name two examples of when you felt isolated in mothering.
2. Where do you crave guidance? Start praying for God to send someone to meet that need.
3. Are you hesitant to ask another mom for help? What barriers do you think keep you from asking for help?
4. In what two areas of mothering do you desire a mentor's help?
5. Who are some moms in your already existing relationships that could serve as good mentors in these areas, even if only through careful observation?
6. Who do you think "Titus 2" women are, according to Paul? Are they family members, women of the church, etc.?

Let's Get Cookin'

- **Start small.** Text a friend and tell her you'll call her tonight after the kids are in bed. Keep the conversation positive.
- **Identify two safe mentors.** Make plans to spend time with them over the next two months. Don't be afraid to be spontaneous. Sometimes less than twenty-four hours' notice will work better than a month's. Work around your children and maximize small windows of free time.
- **Do you have any unsafe people in your life?** Scale back your interaction with them in order to make more time for positive people.

Section
IV

Mothering With
Wisdom and Grace

Chapter 10
Satisfying Self-Care

Mothering places enormous demands on our time and energy. They're cute little demands, but demands nonetheless. How we take care of ourselves determines how much we can ultimately give to our families. No one can give from an empty bucket. Filling that bucket takes intention and a plan. Sure, being a mom means sacrifice. And a reasonable degree of sacrifice is character and compassion building. However, motherhood can't become chronic martyrdom. Otherwise, it defeats God's purpose. The only thing worse than an empty bucket is one overflowing with resentment. We have to recognize when we've crossed the line from healthy sacrifice to soul-draining martyrdom. Usually our attitude toward our husband and children is a good clue of the condition of our heart.

Melinda

"You need to come to my office as soon as you can. I don't want to discuss it on the phone." My doctor's voice was firm and concerned. I quickly drove over, gripping the steering wheel with sweaty palms. I hadn't been feeling well for months. I was tired right down to my bones. My chest felt tight. I was easily short of breath. My hair was like straw and falling out with alarming frequency.

After a scary episode where I felt like an elephant was stepping on my chest, I finally went to the doctor. He did a full battery of tests. The results were in. With grave seriousness, the doctor explained that my thyroid was out of whack and my hemoglobin was so low that he called the laboratory and asked them to re-check my blood for leukemia. Thankfully, it was negative. But that didn't mean I was out of the woods. He looked me in the eye and said firmly, "You're great at taking care of everyone else. Now it's time to take care of *you*."

> The only thing worse than an empty bucket is one overflowing with resentment.

Everything had to stop. I had demoted the priority of my well-being for quite some time. Now, thanks to a health crisis, it had just gotten a promotion.

Good self-care honors our families. We're more available and better equipped to handle all that life throws at us. We can still keep a spirit of humility, giving all the while. Earlier in the book, we talked about aligning our priorities. This is definitely a key component of self-care. The goal is to be patient and loving with ourselves so we can extend grace and love to our families.

Redefining "Me Time"

Moms need some "me time." We've both discovered that "me time" doesn't have to be hours of time. It just has to be consistent. Lunch with a friend. A walk in the evening. Even just a fifteen-minute solitary retreat to your bedroom! Combined with your daily time with God, this makes such a difference in perspective and state of mind.

A break doesn't have to be complete alone time. It doesn't have to be a crazy girls' night out. It can be anything that lightens our mental and physical burdens. Maybe that means hiring a teenager who can play with the kids while we pay bills, clean the kitchen, or do any of the tasks that are difficult with little ones in tow. Or taking the kids to the gym and using the facility's child care while we're working out. Even having our husbands or family members take and/or pick up the kids from school one or two days a week. Those seemingly small reprieves, if we get them regularly, can make a huge impact on our mental and physical energy.

We have to be lovingly assertive and specific about expressing our needs. Our husbands, sisters, moms, mothers-in-law, and friends can't help us if they don't know what we need! Being resentful and silent doesn't bring us any closer to "me time." Neither does venting to our girlfriends. It just guarantees more crazy time. We also run the risk of believing that no one is willing to help us. That's simply not true. Over the past twenty years, we've both found that the only needs a mom has that go unmet are the ones that aren't expressed to loving people.

Practical Ways to Steal Some Time for Ourselves

Rest when the kids do. It's very tempting to "be productive" during naptime or even late at night after the kids are in bed. However, here's a word of caution: Use this time wisely and frugally. Spending this time rejuvenating ourselves during the day and/or getting the rest we need at night can be the difference between wellness or exhaustion. In the long run, we'll get more done and be less irritable.

Plan ahead for dinner. Let's face it. Preparing meals is stressful. Especially when kids have evening activities. A little pre-planning can cut back on the crazy. Find places that offer curbside takeout, or buy ready-to-eat foods from the grocery store that give you time: rotisserie chicken, frozen pizza, pre-cut vegetables, bagged salads. Keep an eye out for coupons or specials.

Redefine "time away." Part of the problem with getting "time away" is that we feel guilty doing it when we know things need to be done. "Alone" time can be at the grocery store. Shopping without little ones can practically feel like a spa day for a mom. Picking out apples in the produce section without any of them being used as baseballs feels luxurious. If you do the bills for the family, why not take the task to a local coffee shop? What peace! Finding a combination of must-do tasks and away-from-home locations that works well for you can help relieve any guilt of getting away. Doing it consistently is what's truly important.

> The only needs a mom has that go unmet are the ones that aren't expressed to loving people.

Build supportive relationships. The "I'll scratch your back if you scratch mine" concept can go in so many directions. We have a habit of calling each other and saying, "I'm going to Target, do you need anything?" We have personally rescued each other from mascara, toilet paper, and stir-fry sauce emergencies, and saved each other precious time. Or we can make a double batch of a meal, freeze it, and offer it when a friend is having a tough week. It takes just a little extra time and money, and builds reciprocating relationships that can give us support and much-needed breathing room now and then.

Make it easy on your "me time" helpers.

Kathy

I found a rather sneaky way to get a hot bath by bathing with my babies and toddlers. Before any of our toes ever hit the water, I was smart enough to lay everything out for Ben so that he could easily whisk them away for diapers and pajamas. Then I got an extra five to ten minutes (the equivalent of three hours to a mom of young ones) to heat up the water in the tub and soak. Ben got to hold a fresh-smelling baby and eventually a fresh-smelling wife, too. It was a win-win.

When we want a little time for ourselves, we should make a few preparations ahead of time to make our helper's job easier.

Think of it as sweetening the pot. It means they'll be more likely and hopefully more than willing to help out again!

Knowing When to Say "Whoa!"

Taking care of our temples is important—resting, eating healthy, and exercising. But let's move beyond the superficial and delve into some of the more subtle ways we drain our buckets. Heart and character issues, such as poor boundary-setting and enabling, can sabotage our joy and energy for mothering.

Setting boundaries as a mom can't be done on the fly. We have enough unexpected challenges.

Recognize that sometimes okay is good enough. If we can't do it perfectly, we often feel like we don't want to do it at all. But we have found that it's much healthier to adopt a philosophy of, "God knows I'm doing the best I can, and that's enough." Perfectionism steals time from us because we become paralyzed by the thought of not getting it all done well, all the time. It leaves us feeling poorly about ourselves. How do we let go of perfect? It's not easy. We believe it's a matter of going back to our goals and priorities.

For example, let's say our child is about to mark his fifth birthday. What's our goal? It should be for our child to feel loved and appreciated. To celebrate his life and place in our family. That can be accomplished without an expensive, stressful, over-the-top extravaganza. It's not about us or impressing others. A simple, small gathering is enough to meet our goal.

Eliminate enabling. Our natural inclination as mothers is to rescue our kids from pain and frustration, to make things easy, happy, and pleasant for them because we love them. But realistically, it's not all about them. We're trying to avoid our own pain of watching our children struggle, fail, or learn something new. It protects *our* image and/or helps *us* avoid conflict and disappointing our

143

children, which makes *us* feel better—*for the moment.* Another unusual area of self-care we need to examine is where we might have created learned helplessness or enabled anyone else we love. From kids to husbands to other extended family, if they can do it for themselves, encourage them to do so. Trying to do everything our own way is not going to buy any time for self-care. Codependence helps no one.

Setting boundaries as a mom can't be done on the fly. We have enough unexpected challenges.

Beware of being overcommitted. It's okay to say no a lot when you have young children. In fact, it's quite acceptable to say no when you have older ones, too. It's healthy. Liberating. And doesn't require an explanation. "No, I'm sorry. I can't," is completely sufficient. We're not required to say anything after that. Really. Some moms enjoy and thrive with a high level of activity. It's just how they're wired. But all moms need to be cautious about taking on too many commitments. Just because we can do lots of things well doesn't mean we should.

Melinda

When I first began to tackle my people-pleasing problem, I agonized over saying no but knew I needed to do it. Often. I began easing myself into this new habit by saying, "Let me get back to you on that," when someone asked me to do something. That way I was able to make a decision at my own leisure without the pressure. "Yes" had been my knee-jerk response for so long that I needed the space to formulate a healthier, God-driven answer.

As a women's ministry director, I'm in a position to ask young moms to volunteer. I try very hard to remember how hard it was for me to say no to these kinds of opportunities, even when I knew my family would suffer. It feels good to be recognized for our talents and leadership abilities! My family suffered many times while I pursued that ego boost and chased others' approval. As a result,

Lovin' Spoonful

Practical Ways for Moms to Eat Healthy on the Run

- **Keep fruit front and center.** You're more likely to grab a small bunch of grapes than keep going hungry.
- **Splurge on healthy prepared foods at the grocery store.** Cut back on other items that don't save you time and energy. Those pre-chopped veggies are more likely to get eaten by a mom on the go than a huge head of broccoli that needs to be washed and cut up.
- **Cook once, eat two or three times.** Today's dinner can become three or four portions of a microwavable lunch if you save meal-sized portions and freeze them.
- **Smoothies.** These make a great handheld snack for moms on the go.
- **Skip soda.** It's so easy to grab a cold can of soda. Make it just as easy to do the same with flavored seltzers and water.

I offer opportunities to young moms, but I also caution them to keep their family ministry first. Recently, I asked a young mom to co-lead a Bible study. She was torn between her desire to lead and the current demands of her busy family. I could immediately relate and assured her that the time would be right later. I could sense her relief. She hugged me and said, "Thank you so much for understanding and giving me the grace I needed to say no without feeling guilty."

The Consequences of Neglect

The consequences of neglecting self-care are huge. It's not just the mother who's cut off at the knees—it's the whole family. That's why taking care of ourselves is, indeed, not selfish. If we allow ourselves to become a burden or liability to our family—now, that's selfish. As moms, we can think we're being noble by being too sacrificial. But what good is an irritable, stressed-out mom? All that good we think we're doing is more of a liability than an asset for our families. Tough, but true.

Sometimes the evidence of neglect slaps us in the face . . . with a disturbing phone call from our doctor. Or it can be a silent, slowly progressing erosion of our well-being.

Kathy

Let's look at depression, an issue close to my heart. For most moms, it sneaks up on us. Thin layers of darkness accumulate slowly. It's not as if one day we say, "Gosh, I'm a wreck. Where is the phone so I can call and get some help?" Yes, I had several clarifying moments, but I ultimately had to make the tough decision to get treatment. I wasn't surrendering to depression. In fact, God helped me attack it. My problem was no longer just my problem. It became my whole family's problem. I had a moral responsibility to get treatment and help. Otherwise, I wasn't serving anyone. I was letting an illness control my life and the lives of those I loved.

If we've gone too long without self-care, things can go very wrong. We might have a tendency to binge. With everything from

 Lovin' Spoonful

Computer and Internet use, either for work or recreation, can be draining. Setting limits is healthy for us and our families. A simple trick is to let the battery run out on our devices. That's right. Unplug it, literally. When the battery runs out, computer time for the day is done.

food to time away, moms can feel so deprived that we're sent into an involuntary tailspin.

I had such an experience when one of my kids was a baby. I went to the store after Ben got home from work to pick up something. I was beyond exhausted. The day had just killed me. Sure, I was being responsible. I was running an errand. But on the drive home, I began having some very irresponsible thoughts. I wanted to run away. Not like a teenager who didn't like her parents, but just run away to be—away.

The consequences of neglecting self-care are huge.

I glanced down at my wallet and saw my glossy little ticket to freedom, a credit card with a substantial limit. I could surely have a night away at a nice little hotel, right? I could order room service. I could sleep for hours . . . and hours. . . . I was about twenty miles away from home when reality hit me in a very primal way. *I'm breastfeeding. I have no pump. Ben has very little milk at home. The baby hasn't even taken a bottle very well yet.* These thoughts prompted me to quickly turn the car around. My husband seemed awfully relieved to see me. I didn't discuss the thoughts from that night for years. Instead, I tried very hard to avoid the situation that led to all of those unhealthy feelings.

Sometimes we have a hard time articulating our needs to someone else, let alone explaining how they can help us. So how do we figure it out? We can start by making a specific list of tasks that overwhelm us or times when we regularly find we're stressed. Then, we can put a check mark by those tasks that only we can do. That list is often smaller than we think. Look at those tasks on your list that can be done by others. Then brainstorm who can help. This often requires a generous helping of humility. Maybe your child is having a struggle—riding their bike, doing math homework, potty training—and you're not able to help them over the hurdle. Enlisting outside help or advice might be the best thing for you and the child.

Hiring tutors has been some of the best money we've ever spent. It's helped our children and preserved our relationship with them. The goal is for our children to be successful; we don't have to be the ones to make it happen in every experience. When we realize that, asking for assistance can be a little easier.

A myriad of psychological and psychiatric issues can wreak havoc on moms and their families. Depression, mood/anxiety disorders, and attention disorders all become much, much worse when they're ignored, even if they were maintained relatively well prior to having children. Moms who suffer through these trials need extra support. We have to do our best to think of our own mental health as being as important as the health of our children and families. Seeking help, sometimes professional, in these critical areas is not optional. It's a requirement.

Is It Selfish or Is It Self-Care?

Can self-care ever become selfish for a mom? Well, sure. We're called to "love our neighbor as we love ourselves," not "treat yourself and forget about everyone else." But where's the line?

Here are a few good questions to ask that can help us determine if our self-care is selfish or not:

Is it an appropriate request?

Kathy

Deciding whether the level and nature of help we're asking for is appropriate is important. Early in his medical career, Ben was on call 24/7 for nine months straight. This was not a good time for me to ask him for a girls' night out, even if I deserved it. Which I did. But that's where baby-sitters helped. It wasn't appropriate for me to ask him to fill that need. Someone else could do that for me.

Children are also completely capable of doing things beyond what we normally expect of them. In order, this is how old each

Lovin' Spoonful

When children want to play sports or participate in other activities, consider your answer carefully. Remember, it's not just two practices and a game a week; it's sixty to seventy hours over a few months. If you can carpool and still have Sundays to rest, then it becomes much more reasonable.

of my children were when they took over doing their own laundry: eighteen, sixteen, thirteen, ten. Notice a trend? I realized way too late in the game that I needed to delegate more in order to feel burdened with less.

Melinda

Some requests *are* unreasonable, but for many years I assumed that *most* requests were unreasonable. It was another symptom of my people-pleasing problem. I never wanted to rock the boat or ask anything of anyone else. In my mind I'd make excuses like *She must be too busy* or *He's probably too tired.* For every excuse I made, a counselor I saw told me to follow that thought with the question, "What's the worst that can happen?" They might say no, but they'll most likely say yes. With my kids, who I hadn't asked much of for a long time, I had to start small. One night, I just simply asked them to rinse and load their dishes in the dishwasher. They did it without a peep. I gradually built from there, empowered by the small victories. I realized my kids—and others in my life—were not only capable of helping me—they were willing! And I was underestimating them.

To the degree that it's possible, minimizing the inconvenience to others helping us is kind. It doesn't take that much effort. For example, if we want our kids to participate in after-dinner cleanup, we can make sure the dishwasher is empty. We can clean up and put things away as we're cooking. If we want our husbands to take the children to school in the morning, we can make sure they're up and ready on time. This kind of pre-planning honors others' assistance and allows us to accept help without guilt. Of course, there are times when we moms just need rescue, but often we can plan ahead so helping out is easier for others.

Does our self-care request interfere with our other priorities? Self-care is vital, but if placed in front of a higher priority like our marriages or our relationship with God, it's counterproductive. A little retail therapy (aka shopping), for example, is fine, unless it's sending us into debt. Dinner with a girlfriend is great, unless we're leaving our family without a plan for *their* dinner. That kind of self-care is not worth the stress and sacrifice of our husbands and children.

In other words, we've learned that self-care has to be intentional for moms. The price is much too high if we neglect ourselves. Making our needs known and keeping them a priority is well worth any effort. We benefit by staying effective, healthy, and happy. Our families reap the rewards of having a mom who is well and can give them what they need.

> All us mommies always want to put our kids first, but if we don't take care of ourselves, we are leaving our kids to a scary future. I have to remind myself of that all the time.
>
> —Savannah, mother of one

Stirring Your Thoughts

1. What is on your "must do" list? What is essential for your mental and physical well-being?
2. In what area(s) is it most difficult for you to say no? Why?
3. On a scale of 1 to 10, how well do you take care of yourself?

4. Do you have difficulty asking for help? Why?

5. Are there any health issues, mental or physical, that need more attention in your life?

6. What tasks are you doing for your children that they should and could be doing for themselves—for their own good and yours?

Let's Get Cookin'

- Pick one aspect of self-care in which you've been procrastinating, like a doctor's appointment. Make a plan today to address it. Ask someone to keep you accountable to follow through.

- Ask your family what are two things you're currently doing for them that they could be doing for themselves. Is there anything they would rather do for themselves? Is there a skill that needs to be taught so that they can? If so, lovingly teach them to do it!

- Find someone to be accountable to for taking better care of yourself. Maybe this is a person who exercises with you. Perhaps it's your husband. Ask them to check in on you at least weekly and see how you're progressing toward a particular self-care goal.

Chapter 11

Valuing Your Role

Moms are like thermostats. We set the tone and temperature in our homes. Our influence will be felt for generations. This can either inspire and motivate us toward more godly character, or send us into the fetal position! Don't worry, though. We're not on our own! We both take great comfort in the assurance that God "has given us everything we need for a godly life through our knowledge of him who called us by his own glory and goodness" (2 Peter 1:3). He also promises us that if we need wisdom (who doesn't?), we "should ask God, who gives generously to all without finding fault, and it will be given to you" (James 1:5).

That dependence on Him empowers our journey. Left to our own devices, we'll lose our focus on the healthy ways we can impact our families. Making the most of our influence will stretch and challenge us. It will bring us to a new level of humility and dependence. When submitted to God, our brokenness can be transformed into something beautiful and beneficial for our families and for us.

Getting Some Respect

We hold a special, highly valued place in our children's lives that can't be replaced. However, we diminish the respect others have for us if we're inconsistent, lack follow-through, or chronically lose our temper. We've both been guilty of this at one time or another. Perfection isn't required to gain our families' respect. What a relief, right? However, humble self-examination and repentance at every turn are critical to gaining it. Our children will respect and learn from our imperfect journey, as well as our willingness to admit our mistakes and ask for their forgiveness. "Love covers over a multitude of sins" (1 Peter 4:8), and "His compassions never fail. They are new every morning" (Lamentations 3:22–23). Can we get an Amen?!

> Perfection isn't required to gain our families' respect.

We can also place ourselves low on the family ladder by not properly claiming our honorable role. We've both realized that we always make sure we get our kids to all their sports and after-school activities. They don't lack for exercise and social opportunities. However, we're not nearly as consistent at scheduling "mom" activity—like taking a walk, working out at the gym, or spending time with friends. Maybe if we called it "soccer practice," that would change! If we don't take care of our needs and value ourselves as we should, what message are we sending to our kids about our worth? Or, let's think about the mom who rarely sits down to eat the very meals that she has lovingly prepared. Mothers have the right to sit down! If we don't, we often won't be treated as respectfully as we should. Taking our place of honor at the family table can be a visual reminder to our children and family that we're steadfast in valuing ourselves right along with them. We can lovingly assert our own worth and value by how we behave.

Valuing our role as God does, setting a positive example, and staying true to our biblical principles gives us extraordinary power in our homes. If we've built credibility and trust with our families, our hard work can also buffer our inevitable failures and mistakes. That's comforting, isn't it?

Lovin' Spoonful

"Psalm 37:1 encourages you not to 'fret because of evildoers.' Instead of worrying or trying to solve every problem in your own power, devote yourself to raising godly children. The power of evil is helpless against the power of the truth you plant in your child's heart and mind. You are a courageous, loving mom when you place your confidence—and your child—into God's care."[1]

Who's Really in Charge?

Ultimately, God should be placed in charge of our lives. We're called to submit to Him (James 4:7). With all of the responsibilities that come with having a family, someone has to exercise full authority. Everything in a family can't be decided 50/50; that thought is a complete delusion. It sounds good, but it doesn't work in the day-to-day reality. We're all on the same team, but every team needs a captain. And in order for someone to be in charge, there has to be someone who *isn't*. Satan has deceived so many of us into thinking that if we're not in charge we're powerless—and being treated unfairly. Giving respect and honor to the father of our children actually takes more strength and gives us more power than keeping our feet in cement and our opinions in overdrive.

Moms tend to spend more time with their children than dads. This can lead to our thinking that we always know better. And guess what? Sometimes we do. Sometimes we don't. The tendency can be to just take over and shut Dad out of the parenting process. That's passive aggression. When we do this, we're being manipulative. What does this look like? Here's an example: We find out one of our children has misbehaved at school but decide not to share it with their father. We think he'll overreact or handle it differently than we'd like, so we keep him out of the loop. We've both been guilty of this. This approach may be easier in the short term, but it's dishonest. Don't think this goes unnoticed by the kids.

More than that, a dad on the sidelines is not good for them. Every single time we include Dad in the process of parenting, in any area, it pays dividends for the whole family. It's the exclusion of them that's more disrespectful and disabling. When we assume they can't do things our way or as well as we can, that ultimately places us in a more vulnerable position. Our goal as moms should be to encourage them not to be fathers that "help" (as if child-rearing is all of our responsibility), but rather fathers that "do."

> We're all on the same team, but every team needs a captain.

If we partner and include them, we give them votes of confidence and encourage them to be men worthy of holding in high esteem. Married fathers who feel honored and respected are more likely to return the same toward their wives. In Ephesians 5:22–23, we learn that husbands are responsible for loving us just as Christ loved the Church. He died for the Church! This directive to husbands certainly gives us a clear idea of just how much Christ loves and honors us and our role. But what if our husbands don't love us in this way? Let's face it. It's a tall order. We realize we don't have control over them, but we can influence and impact them and their behavior.

Scripture tells us that if our husbands aren't "obeying the Word," we can lead by our godly example, enabling the power of the Holy Spirit to "win them over" (1 Peter 3:1–2). The Holy Spirit can work through our obedience to lead our husbands closer to Christ. Isn't that the message of Christianity? It's in our humility—not a demand of "our rights"—that we find true strength. Jesus is the ultimate example of this. We're not about to say this is easy or that change happens overnight—or at all. There are no guarantees. But we can be 100 percent certain that anger and bitterness will do nothing to change our husbands' hearts. And it will only make ours colder.

When men seem uninvolved in some of these areas, it can appear as if they're not worthy of respect. However, if we want dads to engage more in certain situations, let's give them opportunities to do so! Criticizing or minimizing their efforts only leads to alienation and resentment. We should speak up and assert our opinion about how we'd like them to be involved, but we can do it without making our husbands feel stupid or demeaned.

> It's in our humility—not a demand of "our rights"— that we find true strength.

What happens when children are in charge? It can mean more than giving in to their demands. Sometimes we also put them in charge of our feelings or emotions. They don't want that role, and it's completely unfair to give it to them. Our contentment should not hinge on their behavior or approval. True peace can't come from any human being. Its only source is God.

Kathy

I have long had the problem of allowing my emotional well-being to hinge on the approval of one or more of my children. If they liked me on any given day, I felt happy. When they were inevitably discontent with me, my mood would suddenly become gloomy. I had to learn a bit of detachment in order to stay healthy and actually be able to mother them effectively. This became especially difficult as they got older. They were just trying to grow up. I needed to understand that I had to be the grown-up in order to do any good.

What Am I Supposed to Do?

Many times we compound our own stress by taking on responsibilities that aren't ours. By doing this, we're doomed to feel inadequate. We also rob others of their potential in a role or opportunities. Keeping this in mind, it's important to focus on the basics of a mother's responsibilities:

Lovin' Spoonful

These commandments that I give you today are to be on your hearts. Impress them on your children. Talk about them when you sit at home and when you walk along the road, when you lie down and when you get up. Tie them as symbols on your hands and bind them on your foreheads. Write them on the doorframes of your houses and on your gates.

Deuteronomy 6:6-9

Spiritual formation of children. This is more than taking them to church. It's exposing them to the Bible and prayer and helping them form a good conscience. We play a primary role in helping them apply biblical truths to everyday living. They need the freedom to make mistakes, pay consequences, and reap rewards (age- and child-appropriate). It allows them to experience God's grace, mercy, and faithfulness firsthand. We cheat them of something by making life too easy. How will they see their need for God if we're continually rescuing them?

Leading by example. The best way to begin strong spiritual formation in a family is to lead by example. Just how important is our example? For starters, our daughters look to us for how they should embrace their feminine identity. We have the opportunity to show them what modesty and kindness look like. We also hold a special place in our sons' lives, modeling how respectful and loving women should be toward them. We theoretically become the voices our kids hear in their heads: about morality, about themselves, and about the world.

We also set an example by keeping our standards for them high, even when they're fighting us at every turn. We can't give up. We can't treat them like they just can't do it. Godly values will be

157

important their entire lives. We're their moms. If we're not going to hold them to high standards, who will?

Positive forward thinking. Difficulties, character issues, and damaging behaviors don't develop overnight in our children. Neither do positive qualities like work ethic, biblical worldview, and purity. We have to always be looking ahead, mindful of where our kids are now and where the path they're on will take them. We have to be visionaries. By providing constant redirection and correction, we also protect them from themselves until they're able to do so.

Bridge-maker. As moms, we connect all relationships within the family to each other. Here is where we have a choice to become a barrier or a bridge between our husbands, extended family members, siblings, and children. We can promote understanding and relationship by essentially getting out of the way rather than solving every problem, initiating communication, or taking sides. From arranging play dates to participating in charitable activities, our diplomacy as we navigate these interactions helps our children engage with the world.

 Lovin' Spoonful

Insert the name of your child(ren) as you pray this prayer, based on Colossians 1:9-13:

> Thank You for entrusting these precious children into my care. I pray that You will grant them complete knowledge of Your will. Bless them with all spiritual wisdom and understanding. I pray that my children will always honor and please You, Father. May their lives produce every kind of good fruit. All the while I ask that they will grow to know You more deeply. Through Your power, give them the endurance and patience they need. May they always be filled with gratitude toward You. Amen.

Prayer warrior. We strongly believe that, this side of heaven, we won't know the powerful influence our prayers have on the lives of our children. It's another place to wield our power in Christ in their lives, submitting their lives to God and praying for their protection. We love praying Colossians 1:9–13 (see "Lovin' Spoonful" in this chapter) over our children because it covers everything we moms could possibly want for our children. And since it's Scripture, we can be confident that it is God's will for them, too.

Does My Responsibility End?

> As moms, we connect all relationships within the family to each other.

It's hard not to feel overwhelmed by all of the responsibilities involved in mothering. Children will keep pushing against our rules and standards. We have to be the one thing that's unmovable. They need us to be the calm, steady presence in the storms of their lives. We can't get too comfortable. We're their First Responders. This takes every bit of courage we have, through Christ, to believe that we can not only protect them, but also rescue them appropriately. By spending time with them, investing in them, and knowing exactly what's going on in their lives, we're strong enough to address problems as they occur, not after it's a tragedy.

There can be an automatic assumption that if a child is doing something wrong they simply haven't been parented well. Or that every good and right thing they do is somehow a result of supreme parenting skills. If we're honest, fear of judgment is in the back of every mother's mind. Without guidance and a good model, we'll struggle in knowing how to gauge appropriate expectations for our kids. If expectations are too high, our kids break down rather than rise up to meet them. Too low? They become coddled and believe they can do nothing for themselves without help. We usually don't know where the line is. We'll never know unless we watch them struggle a bit, or succeed, and adjust our level of involvement and support.

If we don't know where or when our responsibility ends as a mom and when our child's begins, it can result in our enabling them. Couple that with the fact that children are so different from one another, and we have an even larger challenge. Our responsibility lies in providing a consistent example, setting and communicating boundaries, and telling them the truth often and in the best way we know how. We also have responsibility in how we respond to our children's inappropriate behavior—not ignoring, enabling, or making excuses for their mistakes. Often, it's easier to ignore bad behavior and pretend it's going to blow over. Courage and consistency are crucial to our jobs.

> There can be an automatic assumption that if a child is doing something wrong they simply haven't been parented well.

However, we're called to wield our power of influence appropriately and be humble at the same time. Respect, honor, and responsibility are some of the holiest aspects of motherhood. They're also the most elusive to achieve. We're still called to it. Every moment we surrender to God, every time we seek mercy and forgiveness, He honors the desire of our hearts, every day (1 Peter 2:9; 1:14–16).

God gives us so many choices. Aim for God's best. As I was raising my children, I prayed that God would show me what was best for me and my children in every circumstance. When I was seeking God's guidance this way, it didn't matter what others thought of my choices.

—Marilyn, mother of five

Stirring Your Thoughts

1. How do you think the way you were treated as a child impacted how you view your role as a mom?

2. Where do you sit at your family's dinner table? Do you sit?

3. Who would you like to take more responsibility in raising your children? Your husband, your parents, your church? Why do you feel this way?

4. Do you let your children take charge of controlling your emotions? How can you change this?

5. When it comes to spiritual formation of your child(ren), how are you modeling biblical truths?

6. Where do you feel you could show your kids more of God's love?

7. What relationship in your child(ren)'s lives could use some bridge building on your part? Where can you help promote relationship on their behalf to other family members or other influential people?

8. Where in your mothering have you assumed too much responsibility for your children's actions or behaviors? In other words, where are you a bit obsessed about your influence?

9. Where do you need to assume more responsibility and respond better? Where are you ignoring bad behavior, hoping it will just go away?

Let's Get Cookin'

- Raise one white flag of surrender today to Jesus. Tell Him you're seeking mercy and forgiveness in one area of your mothering. Feel His peace. Rest in His righteousness, not your own.

- Look forward three years in each of your children's lives. How can you be a visionary for them now? Where can you show them all that life can hold for them? Either write this down for your child to read or have a conversation tonight.

- Reach out to someone who needs to know his or her important role in your child's life. Call them or text them.

Keep them informed about the happenings in their life. Even small things can substantially improve the understanding they will have about your child. Ask them to pray for your children after they've had a bad day at school, or let them know the awards your child has won recently. All of these build connection.

Chapter 12

Creating Home

Our life priorities are reflected in how we create our family home. Daily family living within our blessed walls provides opportunities for us to show compassion, build relationships, teach responsibility, and exercise gratefulness for the home we've been given. The chores will get done. The meals will get served. We need to remember to make room for love, flexibility, and grace for ourselves and our families.

The terms *house* and *home* aren't interchangeable. We don't use the expression "House, Sweet House." The house is the physical structure. Taking care of the house includes the care and maintenance—changing the light bulbs, scrubbing the toilets, and fixing the leaks in the roof. Creating a home, on the other hand, involves creating closeness, not just cleanliness. It's the emotion, warmth, and environment that are combined inside of it.

Habits That Keep Things Humming

Discipline (not perfection) in home care and organization can show a good, strong attitude of gratefulness. We generally want to maintain enough good order to allow us to function well and have a healthy family atmosphere. We also want to make spending time together a priority.

Cleaning and organization of a home mostly serve to prevent and keep frustration at bay. It can take time and effort to learn those places and spaces that help or hinder our families' health and happiness, but it's always worth the pursuit.

The state of our surroundings can often give clues to our families' emotional and spiritual health. For example, a chronically disorganized home may be telling us that the family is doing too much. If things are spiraling out of control, it may indicate we're trying to keep too many plates spinning on our own, without depending on others, including drawing on God's power in our lives.

We've found five major strategies that help us more effectively manage our time and space within the walls of our home:

Plan intentionally. Mostly, a mom's job is deliberate, good planning. It's the key to preventing most problems in the home that lead to other larger difficulties. This means being a good manager of our families' time. By planning ahead, we're effectively adding more quality time with our children.

What does this look like? Consider getting up fifteen to twenty minutes earlier than the rest of the family. We know that this can feel like a completely unattainable goal for some, but realize this: Any time we give to ourselves before the family wakes up multiplies our peace tenfold. Fifteen minutes can save an hour of frustration. Creating extra margins of time and space wherever and whenever we can throughout our day allows us to better absorb the "what ifs"—the forgotten homework, the slow checkout line, or particularly grumpy children. This is one place where our anxiety is useful, moms! Planning for worst-case scenarios will actually make everyone much calmer and more relaxed.

Melinda

I know that creating margin, especially in the morning, sounds impossible. I thought it was for years. Kathy tried to convince me otherwise. Finally, my morning routine became so harried, stressful, and difficult that I knew I had to pull out all the stops. So I began getting up before the rest of the family. And it has revolutionized the morning experience—not just for me, but for everyone in the house. Getting a jump start on showering and dressing enables me to be more relaxed. I'm often able to spend time with God while the kids are getting ready. I'm better able to handle the unexpected. It also provided something surprising: It had a trickle-down effect on my kids. They began to get moving a little faster and earlier, too. Everyone was more calm and relaxed. The battles over being late have improved considerably.

> We need to anticipate and plan for what **will** happen rather than what we **wish** would happen.

Some other ways we can create margin are by having a few extra meals in the freezer for a particularly busy week, locking a small amount of emergency money in the car glove compartment, or making sure we're stocked with chicken soup, Popsicles, and Tylenol for inevitable bouts of child and adult sickness. We need to anticipate and plan for what *will* happen rather than what we *wish* would happen. This is a loving and more effective approach. Fighting against reality causes stress and frustration.

Make the space fit your family. Making our physical spaces conform to our families' realities can also make us more relaxed and effective. It requires a change in perspective. Both of us were turned upside down and around in this area.

Melinda

For years, my work-at-home space was pitiful. I occupied a corner of the master bedroom and a tiny, built-in desk in the kitchen. I was uncomfortable, disorganized, and ultimately not productive. Then, one day I looked at my formal dining room, which got used exactly *twice* a year. I was stuffed in a noisy, itty-bitty part of the kitchen, when I had perfectly good space right there for the taking.

Lovin' Spoonful

Choosing to change or modify even a tiny aspect of our home life can have dramatic results. For example, hanging a simple hook for our keys by the front door takes less than five minutes, but that simple act can impact how quickly we get out the door, which makes us more likely to be on time, which keeps us more relaxed—all from a hook on a wall. This kind of positive reinforcement is contagious. We'll seek it again and again. Every time we succeed in shaping parts of our lives to better fit our personalities and lifestyles, our families benefit.

Crazy. I turned my dining room table into my desk. And I bought some inexpensive but attractive bookshelves and file cabinets. Voilà! The room I used twice a year was now getting used every day. I was more effective, relaxed, and productive.

On a similar note, I always had formal couches in the living room. And no one sat on them. *Ever.* So, after nearly fifteen years, I replaced them with more inviting, comfortable couches. Almost overnight, the family began to gravitate to that room to read and do homework. Houses aren't showplaces. They're for *living*.

Kathy

Formal dining rarely happens in my home. When Melinda met me I actually had a Ping-Pong table in my formal dining room—chandelier and all. It made for interesting sound effects and a wonderful laundry-folding table for a family of six! Now there is a piano in there. The formal living room has been sleepover central, a computer room, and a media room. Both rooms have been cleared for a party or two.

Thinking outside the box and changing our environment as our needs and families change and grow is an important way we can make our houses feel like homes.

Do it now instead of later. Let's face it. What we don't want to do now are usually things we don't want to do *ever*. Training ourselves to do it now can be a character-building and stress-relieving exercise. We become more self-disciplined, and it instantly removes the task from our minds and to-do lists. "Do it now" requires less energy than if we decide to put it off for one more second. "Do it now" is more comfortable and kind in the long run. Waiting just prolongs our feeling of unease.

Kathy

I was completely baffled by my dear, naturally tidy friend Claudia. So much so that I decided I was going to shadow her for a morning. I wanted to see how the woman did it. Every time I went over to her house, it was clean. Not just neat—spotless. It drove me crazy. As I sat at her dining room table nursing my baby, I observed the secret. She was making me a snack when something fell on the floor. Miracles upon miracles happened right before me—she bent down and wiped it up, lightning fast.

This may seem like a simple concept to most. For me, it was revolutionary. That simple concept of "doing it now" rather than later can apply to everything in a home. Get a bill in the mail? Pay it. Laundry done drying? Fold it. *Now.* It was revolutionary to someone who literally let things pile up around her for so many years.

> What we don't want to do now are usually things we don't want to do **ever.**

The principle of "do it now" can also apply to controlling clutter. Before we stuff one more thing into an already bulging closet or drawer, it's better to take two or three things out that need to go. The space isn't going to change, but we can change how we view decluttering. It's not an event; it's a habit. It allows our families to better relax and enjoy their surroundings.

Blame systems, not people. What worked yesterday may not work today or tomorrow. We owe it to our families to be flexible and change our methods appropriately when they're not working instead of always assuming *they* should change. If dinner never seems to hit the table before nine o'clock at night, the dinner plan isn't working. We need to look for the hiccup in our routines rather than blame a family member or ourselves.

Kathy

It was very hard not to personalize a system problem when it came to my second son, Paul. I truly believed in the myth that all small children get dressed for school, church, anything, just by politely telling them, "Go get dressed." He was only four, but his brother was able to do this with ease. Paul could not. It was not a personal vendetta he had against me. I had to get creative. So I took pictures of him in various stages of his morning routine and made a photo album to remind him what to do next. I have the cutest pictures of Paul posing while brushing his teeth, putting on his shoes and socks, etc. When I quit *telling* him what to do and gave him a visual, it made all the difference. And I got the best pictures of my four-year-old. My system of saying, "Paul, do this. Paul, do that. Paul, why aren't you doing this? Paul, why can't you do that?" wasn't working. It wasn't his fault, or mine. It was the system.

Melinda

I struggled for years with my kids dumping their shoes, backpacks, and sports equipment at the front door. It made me nuts! I'd get stressed and irritated every time I'd walk by it. Finally, I bought a bench with a lid that has hooks on the back. It's not beautifully organized, but the mess is out of sight. And there's no more nagging.

I know that some would say, "Why don't you just insist that they put their things in their rooms when they walk in the door?" Well, this is one hill that I decided not to die on. I have two teenagers. Long ago, I became well aware that there are more important battles to fight than where they put their cleats. I chose grace instead of nagging. I ended up with less stress, happier children, and a less cluttered space.

Focus on your strengths. Our strengths tend to affect others positively. If we're gifted cooks, our family eats well and feels our love through the food we prepare. If we're great organizers, our family knows where everything is and they are secure in knowing that there is order and control around them.

Where do we shine? When do we feel like we have our best game on? So many times we only want to focus on what we aren't doing well in the area of home care, organization, and management.

Perhaps we're wonderful at organizing and keeping things tidy as can be, but we don't feel like we can cook. Or we're creative types that thrive on spontaneity and struggle to maintain any type of routine. We have to look at the places—even the very, very small places—where we *are* indeed succeeding.

> We need to look for the hiccup in our routine rather than blame a family member or ourselves.

Kathy

For example, I like parties. It taps in to my very social personality. So I use this strength as a motivator to tackle my weakness: keeping my house clean and organized! I used to deliberately ask people over for dinner the same day that I had a really messy house. It was amazing how fast my feet shuffled and things got picked up when I thought someone else would see my mess! Housecleaning by fear! It's also one of the reasons that I have a Halloween get-together every year. I know I will get the house clean for these events. The house is ready for the holidays in the winter by the very nature of having a party. It works for me.

Where Do Kids Fit In?

Our priority is to make sure everything gets done, not do everything ourselves. Our families aren't out-of-town guests. They can and should contribute to the home's well-being! We just need to ask and encourage them to follow through.

Meet Jennifer. She is the mother of five, all under age eight. Two of her children were adopted from an underdeveloped country. After bringing them home and blending their family, she noticed her newly adopted six-year-old making his bed, with carefully folded corners and great attention to detail. Here was a child born in poverty and brought to a loving, secure home, demonstrating how we all should be good stewards of our homes. The other children witnessed his thankfulness and industriousness, as well. "He makes the bed better than I do! I quickly realized how much young children are capable of doing. As parents, we tend to make excuses for them. I was determined not to do that with my kids," says Jennifer.

When giving kids responsibility, the biggest barrier many moms face is the time and patience it takes to teach the skills. Initially, it's easier to do it ourselves. However, as they get older, we keep taking on more and we run the risk of our children becoming lazy and entitled. Jennifer says that the effort of teaching each child the valuable skills is worth it. "I begin by doing a task and having my children watch. Then comes the hardest part. I let them practice the task while I watch," she explains. "This means *only* watching. When they're doing something incorrectly, I give verbal direction. I don't step in and take over. I also give them a list of expectations for each job. No, it isn't perfect, but they're learning life skills."

She then builds a team mentality by having the children inspect each other's work. "*They* check it before *I* check it," she says. "I find they are tougher on each other than I am on them! If they tell me their sibling has done a good job, and they haven't, then the 'inspector' has to fix it and make it right." It's inspiring to us how a loving mother at home implements a Fortune 500 company strategy to increase the family's productivity by reducing micromanagement and encouraging skill-building. The children gain respect for each other and the parent retains ultimate authority.

Kathy

During some critical years for instilling responsible household habits in my children, I struggled with bouts of depression and

Lovin' Spoonful

"Your attitude has to change from 'Why do I have to do this!' to 'This is my home and I deserve to have a wonderful place to live. This blesses my home and my family and, most of all, me!'"[1]

mostly just survived. I wished I had instilled stronger responsibility patterns in them before any tragedy or difficulty came our family's way, but that just didn't happen.

Now that they are much older, this is still behavior that I am undoing at a very slow rate. I find myself getting jealous of other moms who, like Jennifer, have the gift of confident delegation with their children. However, God has revealed to me that what I can do *now* is move forward in obedience, not look back with regret. My older children didn't learn how to do their own laundry until shortly before heading off to college. The two younger ones thankfully have a healthier mom who can challenge and equip them sooner. Only through the help of the Holy Spirit have I been able to turn anything around.

Each family has an individual, unique dynamic. That should always be taken into consideration when deciding appropriate responsibilities. We may have grown up with systems and techniques that just don't gel with our kids' personalities or ours. As we have said multiple times in this book, moms have a choice in what we implement in our households.

Making Adjustments

We have to give ourselves the permission to be flexible. We all have things we need to change about how we manage our homes and families. The approach we use to make these changes should be driven by God's leading and the way He uniquely designed us.

Melinda

Can I be honest? I have major regrets about the level of involvement I required of my children when they were younger. My people-pleasing tendencies and need for control meant that I ended up doing pretty much everything and resenting it. It made no sense. I had chosen not to involve them and yet I was mad at them for not being involved. As they got older, God opened my eyes to how people pleasing was unhealthy for them; I was not equipping my kids. It was a huge epiphany. However, *I* was the only one having this epiphany. My kids weren't seeing the problem with this arrangement. I couldn't expect overnight change in them.

I started with a conversation where I apologized for not involving them more. I told them that it wasn't in their best interest for me to do everything. I explained that I would be expecting more of them in the future. And then I began by asking them to do small tasks around the house, like taking their plates to the sink after dinner or sweeping off the front walkway. At first, there was some pushback. But soon, they actually liked the feeling of being more self-sufficient and independent. It's still not ideal, but it's moving in the right direction. My advice? The sooner you can start giving responsibility, the better. It can be done when they're older, but it is much harder to establish these patterns then.

For me, slow and steady wins the race. If I rushed to change everything in our lives at once, I was probably going to burn out. Picking one small step to take on a regular basis toward a larger goal made sense for me and my family.

For others, the solution to a conflict or need for adjustment may be more swift and drastic. Ruth Soukup, the blogger behind *LivingWellSpendingLess.com*, made a bold move one day—and a very controversial one at that—by removing most of her very discontent little girls' toys and possessions. She witnessed character issues that she knew needed a radical approach. Was she going to be brave enough to follow through on her threat to "take all their stuff away"? One day she did. It all disappeared. The children's

Lovin' Spoonful

And if by grace, then it cannot be based on works; if it were, grace would no longer be grace.

Romans 11:6

reaction was astonishing. At first, they weren't exactly thrilled by the impromptu kidnapping of all their Polly Pockets and Barbie dolls. But ultimately, they benefited even more than Ruth could've imagined. "Taking the kids' toys away provided an enormous amount of clarity about what was motivating and influencing our children. We were rewarded for our courage by the peace we saw them experience after it was done."[2] Over one year later, this act of spontaneous bravery has produced an overall family practice of minimalism.

Now, would that technique work in every family? Maybe for some, but not for all. The most important lesson is to learn what works for you and your family. We sometimes get caught up in wondering why we can't implement someone else's strategies. Working with our own personalities, God-given promptings, and ideas we observe and create will often turn out better in the long run. As with anything in our lives, we will avoid a great deal of frustration if we are continually inviting the Holy Spirit into this process, asking Him what we should do.

It's also important for us to hold back from judging others for what they expect or don't expect of their children. Which family approach is more beneficial for children? It's not our job to determine that for others. Judgment of who's right and who's wrong regarding what their family does or doesn't do must stop. We're called as Christians to love, not to judge. These assessments are often silent, but don't think they go unnoticed by the mom receiving them. This can be incredibly discouraging for moms who struggle with organization or discipline. We don't know the difficulties other moms face. Most likely, we're all trying the best we can. Why don't we compliment each other on what we're doing right? It's amazing what that does for a mom's confidence.

Kathy

I lived under a cloud of judgment for years until I realized that our home was simply not going to look like others'. Ever. Was I giving up on alphabetized cans in the pantry and pillows perfectly fluffed? I prefer to think of it as Jesus giving me a giant hug and saying, "It's okay. Love your kids. The laundry being folded and put away won't get you to heaven."

Judgment of who's right and who's wrong regarding what their family does or doesn't do must stop.

In the Bible, Jesus tells us how to view caretaking in the home. He praises Mary for choosing "what is better, and it will not be taken away from her" (Luke10:42). She recognized that she needed to tend to Him. She showered Him with care and affection. If Jesus finds this behavior more blessed, shouldn't we, as well? That's a difficult proposition when dishes have piled up and the garage is overflowing with junk. But we should be inspired to simplify things to the point that we can keep Him first and still minister to our family with the same attitude that Mary had.

For all those tidy mamas out there, we salute you. We'll never fall into that blessed category; however, we've become more and more comfortable in how we conduct our (messy) lives. We've both chosen to embrace our strengths and work diligently on our weaknesses. We've come a long way, but we'll always have a pile of paper or a little laundry to do. It's taken some time, but we've learned to accept that about ourselves and move on.

Adjusting, learning, and stretching ourselves shows love in action. We're not perfect; we never will be. But consistently trying to improve on caring for our homes and those inside them shows love. Our real goal should be to make our families feel cherished, welcome, and comfortable. It's also an opportunity to help our kids to grow in responsibility, skills, and gratefulness as we involve them in home management. These are far more motivating and worthy goals than a shiny kitchen floor.

> We do "10-minute tidies," where we run around together for ten minutes picking up things around the house. We also take a break between activities . . . and pick up one item for each year of their age. My five-year-old puts away five things; my nine-year-old puts away nine. For myself, I have a few thirty-minute playlists on my iPhone; I plug in some headphones and clean like crazy 'til the music stops.
>
> —Janine, mother of two

Stirring Your Thoughts

1. Make a list of three systems that are working well in your home. What can you learn from them?
2. How inviting is your home when you and your family walk in the door after a long day?
3. What household management tasks are most important to you?
   - To your husband?
   - To your children?
   - How can you make these more of a priority?
4. Where are you struggling the most?
5. How can you apply the principles that help you succeed (question #1) to your areas of struggle?
6. When and where do you show love to your family and your home?

Let's Get Cookin'

- Have an informal meeting with your family. Ask them what they love about your home. Then ask them to be completely honest about what things about home management make them feel stressed and insecure. Focus on just listening without being defensive. Take notes.

- Pick one area of stress and brainstorm some ways to solve the problem as a family.

- Decide on three practical ways you can prepare for the "what ifs" in your family life.

Chapter 13

Feeding Your Soul

Quiet time. What's that? Do you know of any woman who experiences quiet time after she becomes a mother? In our homes, a peaceful moment is about as rare as clean, paired-up socks and sibling civility. But quiet time is what a lot of us call our time with God.

Melinda

When my kids were super small, I remember a well-meaning but misguided older woman at my church telling me, "Don't worry too much about spending time with God when your kids are little. You're so busy. You'll have time later." Perhaps. But would I still have my *sanity*? The demands and responsibility of motherhood meant that I needed God *right then*, and more desperately than ever before.

Staying connected with God on a daily basis isn't only about equipping ourselves for *today's* struggles of sick children, homework battles, or financial stresses. Every time we pray, study God's Word, or memorize a Scripture verse, we're also banking spiritual reserves for *future* circumstances, difficulties, and crises. The consistent focus on applying God's Word to everyday life over many years adds up. Each time, the Holy Spirit works through His Word and speaks to our hearts. This enables us to naturally tap in to supernatural strength, wisdom, and power when life gets tough.

And our example is not lost on our children. Actively pursuing a vibrant relationship with Jesus reaps dividends in our attitudes, our patience levels, and our ability to pass down our faith.

> The consistent focus on applying God's Word to everyday life over many years adds up.

How we *live out* what we say we believe—in our habits, our choices, and how we spend our time—is being intently observed by little eyes and ears. It can be a scary thought. But we can't let the weight of this responsibility condemn or paralyze us. Instead, let's be inspired to make a plan to grow more deeply in love with the Father through a disciplined approach to knowing Him. Our whole family will reap the benefits.

Where Do We Find the Time?

Extra time doesn't get delivered by UPS. As difficult as it seems, we have to be intentional about finding time with God.

Melinda

As a mom of young children, I was known to sit in an empty parking lot to read my Bible. I sometimes locked myself in the bedroom to pray. Grabbed a couple moments of godly wisdom as my bathroom reading. All in a quest to steal a few uninterrupted minutes to pour my heart out to God and allow Him to fill me up. But that wasn't a plan. It was just a young mommy trying to survive.

Kathy

I relied solely on attending Mass on Sundays. It felt like such a Herculean effort just to do that as a mom of little ones. But since I wasn't preparing my heart with regular Scripture study and prayer throughout the week, I wasn't able to effectively apply and internalize Sunday's message.

If we are willy-nilly about our approach, it can only serve as a temporary fix to a greater spiritual hunger. Yes, it can be difficult to integrate spiritual nourishment within the busyness of life, but there's nothing like being fat and happy on the Word of God. Regular time with God doesn't happen if we don't make time for it. It must be planned, deliberate, and routine.

Different stages of motherhood require modification of this routine. Before we had kids, perhaps we were disciplined enough for thirty minutes of quiet time every day. Maybe we've never had any particular routine for our time with God. Once we're moms, we find we need more encouragement than ever from God's Word, but we often struggle to fit it in because of sweet little distractions in the form of chubby cheeks or lunches to be packed. Here are some ways we've found to integrate Scripture, religious books, and other supportive resources into our daily walk with Christ.

Combine it with a daily task. Our job description requires that we're able to juggle multiple tasks. We can apply that skill to incorporating time with God.

If we are willy-nilly about our approach, it can only serve as a temporary fix to a greater spiritual hunger.

Melinda

I had to get creative when it came to when and where I read the Bible. When my kids were babies and toddlers, I read Scripture and/or a devotion during my daily ten-minute hair-drying time. It wasn't as much time as I'd have liked, but I was able to be in the Word consistently. My hair was fluffing while my soul was filling.

Use car time wisely. Having a small Bible or devotional book handy is an awesome way to take advantage of idle time in the car—waiting for a child's soccer practice or dance class to end, idling

Lovin' Spoonful

Invite the Holy Spirit into your Bible study time with this simple prayer:

> Lord Jesus, please open my heart to Your Word and Your Holy Spirit. Help me to recognize Your voice and give me the courage and humility to listen and follow through on Your guidance—even when it's hard and uncomfortable.

in the parent pickup line, or waiting for an infant to wake up so we can go into the grocery store.

Don't be afraid of the dark. As we've suggested earlier, waking up before the rest of the house can give us the reward of something most moms need more of: Quiet. Silence. And, in our experience, quiet doesn't happen once they open their eyes—and their mouths!

The other benefit of morning Scripture study is that we have the entire day to reflect and apply what we've read or heard.

Kathy

For Roman Catholics, daily Mass is a strong part of the tradition. For centuries, believers have started their day by communing with God through Scripture readings, being present with others, and participating in Holy Eucharist. And it's only fifteen to thirty minutes, depending on the priest or deacon. Don't worry about bringing babies and children to church—they're always welcome.

Some of us may find evenings more peaceful—after everyone has fallen asleep. Perhaps *we* even doze off during our devotions. That's okay! What better way to end our day than in the Lord's presence? Even the Little Flower, St. Thérèse of Lisieux, talked about falling asleep during prayer. She said, "I reflect that little children, asleep or awake, are equally dear to their parents." Our

Father God feels the same way toward us mommies when we try to focus and fall asleep.

How Do We Study?

Should we *study* Scripture or just read through it? What's the difference? Reading is the practice of tracking words on a page. Plowing through, if you will. When we slow down and are more intent on comprehension of what we're reading, asking for the Holy Spirit's guidance and bringing in Bible study tools, *that's* studying. Don't let the word *study* intimidate you. Hebrews 4:12 (NLT) says, "For the word of God is alive and powerful. It is sharper than the sharpest two-edged sword, cutting between soul and spirit, between joint and marrow. It exposes our innermost thoughts and desires." A Book that compelling deserves a careful and deliberate examination.

Melinda

I used to go to the Bible mostly for comfort, to feel better. God was gracious to bring people into my life who challenged me to go deeper and be more disciplined. Often, this was *not* comfortable. It required me to face things about myself that I'd rather rationalize or ignore. I had to acknowledge that what God was teaching me through His Word wasn't all about me—it was also so I could use what I'd learned to impact others. Submitting to the promptings of the Holy Spirit, communicated through *study* of His Word, has been worth the sacrifice of "feel good," me-centered Bible reading.

We've both seen the impact of this approach on our relationship with Jesus. It's so much richer. We began to know Him in a way that we never had before. Our faith became who we were, not just a nice set of principles we tried to follow (quite imperfectly, we might add). Over the years, as we've obeyed His promptings and let Him root out dark places in our hearts, thoughts, and attitudes, we've seen this filter into our marriages and parenting in miraculous ways.

As we study God's Word, reading what others have said about Scripture can be valuable and enlightening. Biblical resources should be Christ-focused and help us better understand the historical context and meaning of Scripture. They might include a Bible dictionary, commentaries, or a concordance. Many good sources can be found online. For a list of our recommendations, please see the appendix.

> God honors our desire to know Him and can multiply our small, sincere efforts.

What if we know we should be doing more in our spiritual lives and feel guilty for not doing so? Realize that finding a starting place *anywhere* is valuable. God honors our desire to know Him and can multiply our small, sincere efforts. He's big. He's willing to plant seeds of truth wherever He's invited to grow.

Below are a few methods of study that we've used over the years to study the Word:

Passage by passage.

Melinda

For me, reading an entire chapter at once can be overwhelming and I can easily forget what I've read. I love choosing a book of the Bible and then going through it a passage at a time. One year, using this method, I made it a goal to go through all the Gospels, starting with Matthew. This is a methodical approach to studying God's Word that allowed me to see the "big picture" and follow the Scripture sequentially, rather than focusing on one or two isolated Scriptures that can easily be misinterpreted if they aren't read in context. I usually have a commentary or Bible dictionary handy to look up anything I don't understand or refer to when I need more explanation.

Kathy

Over the last twenty years since becoming Catholic, I personally have experienced how the Liturgy of the Word system helps keep

Lovin' Spoonful

Are you new to Christianity and intimidated by reading the Bible? Start in the Gospels, specifically the Gospel of Mark. Get to know the person of Jesus. Then the Scriptures will all lead to Him. Consider getting *The Action Bible* to read alone and with your children.

Bible study organized. It's mind-boggling to me that the same Scriptures are read and explored throughout the *entire world* on the same schedule. Over the course of three years, including Sunday and weekday readings, 13.5 percent of the Old Testament and 71.5 percent of the New Testament is covered.[1] That's comforting to know for someone who often doesn't feel like she gets anything more than halfway done!

There are many Bible reading plans available. Those organized similar to the Catholic Church's are referred to as Common Lectionaries in many other traditions. Others focus on a particular theme or goal. For example, study Bibles such as *The One-Year Bible* are designed in a devotional format. All of them make reading God's Word less overwhelming and more methodical and intentional.

Organized Bible study. God knows we need each other! Community is essential for support, encouragement, and accountability.

Melinda

As a young mom, I started leading Bible studies when my then-pastor's wife and dear friend asked me to. I thought she was nuts. But she had faith in me. At first I led them because then I knew I would *have* to make time to be in the Word. Now I lead studies as women's ministry director at my church—a position I couldn't have ever imagined having back then. *Leading* studies might not be right for everyone, but be open to God leading you out of your comfort zone to bring you closer to Him. We never know what God might be preparing us for.

Even if we're not feeling called to lead a study, we can benefit so much from gaining support and accountability from other people who also want to go deeper in the Word. During seasons that I couldn't participate in a group study, I've gone through Bible study books on my own. Years ago, I went through a period where most of my time was spent in doctors' offices and therapy sessions. I couldn't commit to group study. However, I worked my way through *Jesus the One and Only*, a Bible study book by Beth Moore, at the same time my church was offering it. At Sunday church and by phone, I discussed what I was learning with friends who were taking the class. It was one of the sweetest study times I've ever had.

Today, fifteen years later, there are many online Bible studies that moms can participate in without ever leaving their homes, while still tapping in to the virtual support and community of other Jesus-loving people.

Use a journal. Prayer journals record prayers and insights that God is giving us through His Word. There's something very freeing about pouring prayers and thoughts out to God on paper. It brings a much-needed release.

 Lovin' Spoonful

Spiritual books help us in our journey toward heaven. Consider keeping these around the house. Some of our favorites include *Mere Christianity* by C. S. Lewis, *My Utmost For His Highest* by Oswald Chambers, and *Streams in the Desert* by L. B. Cowman and James Reimann.

Melinda

I've been able to look back weeks, months, or even years later and see how God has answered prayers and helped me grow as a woman and a mother. Going back to these journals is a faith-building exercise that I've found especially valuable when going through tough times. Seeing His past faithfulness time and time again—both in answering prayer and *not* answering it!—strengthens my belief that He'll give me what I need to face the difficulties I'm having right now.

How Do We Keep Connecting Throughout the Day?

Pray throughout the day. Children watch and follow our example. Incorporating prayer into our day invites the Holy Spirit to work in them, planting seeds that will grow later. Talking to God out loud, boldly, and without reservation tells kids that God is always listening. It invites the Holy Spirit to work in us, as well.

Melinda

When the kids were old enough, I would stop in the middle of whatever we were doing and say a quick prayer with them: "Let's ask God to help Mommy find her keys" (I'm always losing things—seriously, it's a sickness), or "Grandma isn't feeling well. God, will you please help her to feel better?" Over the years, this has helped me to keep the connection going throughout the day, and it helped train my kids to turn to God with their needs—big and small. Now my kids are teenagers, and we still do this. *They* often initiate it, too.

Listen while we work, rest, or play. Here is where the online world can contribute to your faith walk. Most sermons, readings, and books can be portable with smartphones or computers.

Kathy

I'm a big audiobook and podcast fan. I subscribe to the "Daily Readings of the Catholic Church" in audio. I can listen to a week's readings, which lead up to Sunday's Gospel, and stay in the loop of the church's liturgical calendar. Podcasts from various priests, speakers, and authors also encourage me. They're stored for whenever I can listen to them on demand. They can also serve as an alternate family devotional. Sometimes my kids will join me in snuggling up and listening before bedtime. Also, YouTube isn't only for building rock stars. Almost every ministry has a channel providing talks, seminars, and interviews. Look in the appendix for suggestions.

How in the World Can We Make a Difference?

Keeping our spiritual lives active through prayer and Scripture study simply makes us more effective, loving mamas. When we've filled ourselves up, words of encouragement for others come more naturally.

For busy moms, using our time, talent, and treasure for God can look different during the many seasons of motherhood. Sometimes using them well can seem completely out of reach. Time? We don't have much of this. Talent? Maybe we have quite a bit, yet no time to give it. Treasure? Most of it goes toward raising the little pumpkins God has given us.

Meet Carla. She began working in her church nursery when her first child was born, primarily out of guilt. "I felt that if I was using the nursery, I needed to give back and do my part," she says. Three kids and many years later, it's become a full family ministry that has blessed thousands of families. Countless mothers were put at ease with Carla's warm, easygoing, yet capable manner. For some, she was the first person they entrusted their little one to outside of family. Carla will probably never know how many parents were able to hear the Gospel or a life-changing message because they knew their children were in good hands. "My kids grew up and all of them played with the babies right alongside me as soon as they were old enough," she says. "They all have a deep love for children, and through their actions and ministries, it's growing exponentially."

Recently, Carla retired as the nursery coordinator to carry on a longstanding generational tradition of caring for children within her extended family. When her great-niece was born, she became her nanny. "I've watched other godly relatives help care for the little ones in our family, so it just seemed right and natural for me to do this. I have the opportunity to pray with my great-niece, sing, and read her Bible stories."

Melinda

As I've shared throughout the book, I've struggled as a mom for a variety of reasons. Those struggles have fueled my desire to go deeper with Jesus. I need Him so desperately. It also channels my pain and angst into encouraging others. Even though it was difficult to do this when my children were little, teaching those Bible study groups helped take the focus off myself and gave me opportunities to minister to others who were struggling just like me, whether in motherhood, marriages, or some other area of life. I still find this true today.

> Remember, every saint had a mother.

Kathy

The most logical place to do any volunteer work outside of my church or home is my children's school. I enjoyed the community of people I interacted with, and my kids were close. There wasn't a need for child care most of the time. "Christmas Craft Day" for a first-grade class also became a craft day for whichever baby was on my hip! Since my little ones grew up doing these activities at school, it actually made their eventual transition to starting school easier.

Yes, some of us can become missionaries in foreign lands and destitute places. As moms, our first mission fields are our homes. We may not be serving in soup kitchens every week or building aquifers in the rain forest, but we're ministering to those closest to us—our family. Raising kids in a godly manner can contribute just as much to the world's causes and concerns. Remember, every saint had a mother. We can never underestimate the impact we have on those who are watching us make difficult, God-honoring choices as we raise our families. Our witness can be powerful, especially on young women who are observing godly examples of mothering.

As moms, our first mission fields are our homes.

As moms, we have to allow God to fill our hearts with Living Water. Finding regular time with Jesus can be hard. In Luke, Martha complains to Jesus that Mary was at His feet and not helping her in the kitchen. Jesus lovingly reminds her, "Martha, Martha . . . you are worried and upset about many things, but few things are needed—or indeed only one. Mary has chosen what is better, and it will not be taken away from her" (Luke 10:41–42). Yes, laundry and little ones must be cared for, but God will always honor the time we make to sit at His feet.

I have a very active fifteen-month-old and am four months pregnant. I have found myself using my quiet time for naps or showers, and feeling very out of touch with God and guilty for not making enough time in my day for Scriptures or just to talk to God without my mind going in a million different places. I realized that with a few small adjustments throughout my day and some out-loud prayers with my son, I can have a continuous conversation with God—not just a huge spillage of thoughts and prayer lists that I try to remember each night before I fall asleep.

—Kara, mother of two

Stirring Your Thoughts

1. What is your biggest barrier to spending time in prayer and Bible study?
2. Which of the methods in the chapter might work for you, taking into account your schedule and personality?

3. Think back to a time when you were especially close to Jesus. What were you doing then? What practices or habits can you begin again to regain that level of closeness?

4. Brainstorm three ways to increase your Scripture exposure and reading time.

5. What is one way you can be more intentional in your prayer life?

6. If you could serve in any ministry in your church, what would it be?

Let's Get Cookin'

- **Make a devotional basket.** Put your Bible, prayer journal, Bible study book, devotional, pens, etc., in a basket. When the kids are napping or otherwise occupied, you'll be ready to spend some valuable moments with God. If you don't have a Bible, invest in one (or more). Electronic versions for your smartphone or reading device are available in any translation.

- **Pretend your Bible is your cell phone for a couple of days.** Keep it as handy and available. Watch the Holy Spirit move.

- **Set the home page on your computer's browser to an inspirational website.** Proverbs 31 Ministries has daily devotions and Scripture readings (http://proverbs31.org). For Catholics, the USCCB site (http://usccb.org) has the daily readings that correspond to the Liturgy of the Word.

Chapter 14
Depending on God's Power

The mothering journey can be a strong catalyst for our Christian faith as moms. Let's rejoice in the fact that we're not alone in our struggles. Let's embrace it! Thankfully we have Jesus, who has always been there through all our sins and difficulties. Our mothering struggles are no different. He cares.

Through blogging and interviewing for this book, we've noticed how hard it is for moms to examine the heart issues central to the relationship we have with God. He calls us to exercise self-examination, repentance, and forgiveness. Yet it's hard to apply these principles to motherhood. It's easier to see and work on the "sins of the flesh" of mothering—home organization, kids' behavior, etc. They're outward signs of what are supposed to be the good and bad parts of being a mom. But God wants our hearts—not our schedules, pantries, and picture-perfect Christmas cards.

Moving from guilt to grace in mothering our children is only possible through the sacrifice of Christ. It requires us to look up into Jesus' eyes as He tells us to "go and sin no more" (John 8:11 NLT) and we watch all the stones of judgment drop to the ground. We, too, need to drop the stones that we inflict upon ourselves as we journey through our mothering role. They're not fruitful or encouraging, and they hinder our ability to live out God's calling on our lives.

From Fear to Hope

God convicts us of sin and moves us to repentance and forgiveness. He wants to restore intimacy with us. He is always working for our good. However, feelings of *condemnation*, which are not from God, can cause us to move further away from Him. How can we "approach God's throne of grace with confidence" (Hebrews 4:16) when we falsely believe that He's disapproving of us? We can easily begin to look for other sources of validation and fulfillment in our lives.

If we're not careful, motherhood, as beautiful and God-given as it is, can act as a hollow substitute for the only true source of worth and satisfaction—Jesus. When we primarily look to our husbands, our children, or our role as a mom to fill us up, we ultimately come up starving and empty. There's a real danger of making false idols of our families. Our children's accomplishments and opinions of us can become the focus of our worthiness. We burden them with the job of being our measure of effectiveness in the world. Yet nothing else will fill the God-shaped void in our souls. Not even the ones we love so dearly.

> God wants our hearts—not our schedules, pantries, and picture-perfect Christmas cards.

Melinda

When I was a lost child of God, I looked to worldly things and imperfect people to provide validation and comfort that only He could give. The root of my battle with people pleasing was a desire to be "enough." But the bar kept rising. One moment I was mom of the year because my kids were content and happy with me. The next, I felt completely inadequate when they inevitably couldn't give me enough love or approval to fill me up. Other people's opinions and feelings, particularly theirs, became a false idol. They had replaced God as most important to my sense of well-being.

Lovin' Spoonful

Does Jesus know how you struggle as a mom? Yes. He was fully human, yet fully divine. Take heart that He understands even the smallest problems we experience. He gets it. He promises.

Our children's opinions of us change more often than the weather. I had to break free from the fear of disappointing them. It was in their best interest and mine. The only way I could do that was to quit looking to them for my worth. They didn't want or need that responsibility. I became convicted that I had to be even more obedient to God than before I became a mom. I gradually learned that if I was obedient to Christ in my mothering, regardless of how my children viewed me at any given moment, my worth was secure.

One decision at a time, I began to do what was best for my children instead of what was more comfortable for my ego. I daily, moment-by-moment, ask for God's wisdom and courage instead of relying on old habits and my kids' validation to fill me up. This was not an overnight process. In fact, I'm *still* on this journey. However, as I continue to submit to His leading, I'm filled with a peace and courage that empowers me. It's changed everything about my mothering. My kids are no longer in charge of my worth and emotional health. What a relief—for them and for me! My mothering is now motivated by the guidance of their heavenly Father.

From Pride to Humble Pie

Humility grows during struggles and increases our dependence on God. He uses this process to create in us a teachable heart. But that is our choice. We can continue to fight it or we can embrace our brokenness and cooperate with God's guidance and plan.

Kathy

Who was *my* false idol? Myself. After all, I was told by *everyone*, "The only person a woman can depend on is herself!" The '70s and '80s made sure that every cultural experience—from movies to college—centered on that thought. What a crock! That made for a short trip from feeling confident to wallowing in the overwhelming demands of motherhood.

Before I had children, my opinion of what kind of mother I was going to be was amazingly high considering I hadn't even given birth. I related so much to the Pharisee's prayer (Luke 18:9–14). I used to say the same thing about being a mom: Oh God, thank you that I am not like _____! Thank you, God, that I made a choice to avoid _____. All of those shallow, immature thoughts

Lovin' Spoonful

Therefore, since we have been made right in God's sight by faith, we have peace with God because of what Jesus Christ our Lord has done for us. Because of our faith, Christ has brought us into this place of undeserved privilege where we now stand, and we confidently and joyfully look forward to sharing God's glory.

We can rejoice, too, when we run into problems and trials, for we know that they help us develop endurance. And endurance develops strength of character, and character strengthens our confident hope of salvation. And this hope will not lead to disappointment. For we know how dearly God loves us, because he has given us the Holy Spirit to fill our hearts with his love.

When we were utterly helpless, Christ came at just the right time and died for us sinners. Now, most people would not be willing to die for an upright person, though someone might perhaps be willing to die for a person who is especially good. But God showed his great love for us by sending Christ to die for us while we were still sinners.

Romans 5:1–8 (NLT)

ultimately backfired. I wasn't strong enough for *myself.* I was no more secure, nor any better than any other mom.

It took brokenness to realize that I needed to rely on the Lord, my husband, and countless others. My dependency wasn't a weakness. It was just a true admission of vulnerability and a good starting place for God to work on my heart. The more I revealed that I was struggling, the more God blessed me with people faithfully serving Him. I found out that I could indeed "do all this through him who gives me strength" (Philippians 4:13), including being a mom.

We've Got the Power!

On most days, in our own power, we're close to being one tantrum away from having one ourselves. One stressful morning away from turning into a hot mess. We're completely powerless on our own.

> The good news is that Jesus never lets the needs of His children go unmet.

The enemy would love to keep us stuck in these feelings of inadequacy and helplessness.

Remember these words: "My grace is sufficient for you, for my power is made perfect in weakness" (2 Corinthians 12:9). We do have access to power, after all. His name is the Holy Spirit.

We *don't* have to give in to feelings of anger and impatience. We *don't* have to succumb to paralyzing feelings of inadequacy. In Ephesians 1:19–20, we're told that we have the same power available to us as it took to raise Christ from the dead. No matter how challenging we think our children are at times, they don't require more power than *that.* Mostly, it's training our minds and hearts to be more focused on and obedient to Him. Giving our guilt, our fears, our worries to Him.

This requires us to develop the habit of asking Him for help, even with little things. This creates intimacy. It builds our faith as we see Him answer our prayers for help and guidance throughout the day. The more we open our hearts to the Spirit, the more we sense His promptings—those "feelings" that inspire, instruct, and protect us.

When we start asking for the Holy Spirit's power in our lives and in our mothering, be prepared. Satan knows the positive impact it will have on our children and others, and he's going to fight it. Hard. And he doesn't play fair, either. Even though we are surrendering our vulnerabilities to God, Satan is taking notes. Staying under close, continuous guidance is the key to allowing the Holy Spirit to rule.

Apart from God, we'll never be truly satisfied.

His power provides us with the immense love needed to care for our children. It's often hard to remember that *we ourselves* are children, adopted out of pure love. The good news is that Jesus never lets the needs of His children go unmet. He didn't tell the five thousand who were hungry to tough it out, weather through it, and get over themselves. No, He multiplied the blessings that they already had to satisfy them completely (Matthew 6:30–44). We've all got plenty for Jesus to work with, ladies. We have plenty for Him to use and multiply in order to fulfill the mission He gave us through motherhood. It's there just for the asking.

God gives us what we need, when we need it, like He did for the Israelites in the desert with manna. We need to be fed by God. He feeds us through the Bread of Life, His Son, Jesus. When we're fed only by worldly influences and what others think of us, it comes out in our actions, in mothering, or otherwise. We need Him. Feasting our souls on Christ empowers us to be completely satisfied. That's what happens when we finally let Him into our hearts to revolutionize mothering for us. He doesn't shy away.

God provides us with loving guidance through prayer, community, and deepening our understanding of Him. He tells us over and over, "Do not be afraid." We must take Him at His word and keep doing the best that we can to honor Him and our families.

It's Time

Apart from God, we'll never be truly satisfied. When we follow our craving all the way to His feet and accept the free gift of His sacrifice for us, He saves our souls. It's not a one-time choice to seek God instead of our precious young ones to make us feel good about ourselves. It's a daily, sometimes moment-by-moment decision to focus on the truth of what God says about us. His love is not dependent on how good of a mother we are or how well we serve Him. Titus 3:5 tells us, "He saved us, not because of righteous things we had done, but because of his mercy."

Thankfully, He gave us each other to be flesh and blood agents of His love and support. Let's partner with other mothers and gain the reinforcement we need. Are you ready to toss those cookie-cutter formulas and start mothering with confidence and freedom powered by the Holy Spirit? Good! It's time.

It's time to embrace motherhood for all that God intended, and connect to those around us as well as offer it to others. God can redeem our mistakes and guide our future.

It's time to start mothering from scratch—wherever we are. He'll meet us there.

Lovin' Spoonful

Dear Lord,
Thank You for sending Your Son, Jesus.
Thank You for my children.
I ask that You enter my life in the most powerful way only You can,
To strengthen me, to encourage me, and to show me Your will.
Walk alongside me as I mother Your children.
Help me to see them as You see them,
Love them as You love them,
And to show them Your love in return.
Amen.

Stirring Your Thoughts

1. When did you become a Christian? How has that faith journey affected your role as a mom?
2. In three words, like a headline of the front page of a newspaper, describe your journey up to now as a mom.
3. How can Christ change the headline of your life? What will you ask of Him today?
4. What do you believe God has offered you that has been difficult for you to receive? Why?
5. Where in your life do you feel the most hungry for God?
6. Have you ever uttered the Pharisee's prayer (Luke 18:9–14) about being a mom?

Let's Get Cookin'

- **Have you been waiting to fully commit your life to Christ?** Well now is the time, sister. A simple invitation is all He needs. Open the door to your heart. Don't be scared. Just be prepared to experience life as it was truly meant to be, led by the Holy Spirit, with grace, peace, and forgiveness. It's all yours for the asking.

- **Get rid of the junk food that feeds your soul.** Too much of this, not enough of that. Find ways of filling your belly on the goodness of God by reaching out to the Body of Christ around you. They need you as much as you need them.

- **Explain to those who love you that you're getting a little more of Jesus into your life.** Church, Bible study, and prayer are no longer going to belong to others. They will now belong to you. Shine your light for your family to see God's work in your life. Share with them all that He has done.

Appendix

Additional Resources

Bible Study Resources

Jennie Allen. *Stuck: The Places We Get Stuck and the God Who Sets Us Free*. Nashville, TN: Thomas Nelson, 2011.

Sergio Cariello and Doug Mauss. *The Action Bible: God's Redemptive Story*. Colorado Springs, CO: David C. Cook, 2010.

Jeff Cavins, Tim Gray, and Sarah Christmyer. *The Bible Timeline: The Story of Salvation: Study Set Questions*. West Chester, PA: Ascension Press, 2011.

Scott Hahn and Kimberly Hahn. *Genesis to Jesus: Journey Through Scripture*. Ann Arbor, MI: Servant Books, 2011.

Tammie Head. *Duty or Delight? Knowing Where You Stand with God*. Nashville, TN: LifeWay Press, 2011.

iDisciple. www.iDisciple.org.

Shawn Lantz. *Living with Unmet Desires: Exposing the Many Faces of Jealousy*. Nashville, TN: Word Distribution, 2009.

Olive Tree: The Bible Study App. www.olivetree.com.

James Strong. *The New Strong's Expanded Exhaustive Concordance of the Bible*. Nashville, TN: Thomas Nelson, 2010.

Podcasts

The Catholic Lectionary. "Daily Readings from The New American Bible." https://itunes.apple.com/podcast/daily-readings-from -new-american/id206228295?mt=2.

InTouch Ministries. Daily Radio Program with Charles Stanley. https://itunes.apple.com/podcast/daily-radio-program-charles/ id117752146?mt=2.

Living Proof with Beth Moore. www.oneplace.com/ministries/ living-proof-with-beth-moore.

John Piper. Desiring God. www.desiringgod.org/sermons.

Elisa Pulliam. More to Be. www.moretobe.com/category/podcast -videos.

UMD Newman Catholic Campus Ministry. https://itunes.apple .com/us/podcast/umd-newman-catholic-campus/id273537688? mt=2.

Additional Resources

Julie Barnhill. *She's Gonna Blow! Real Help for Moms with Anger.* Eugene, OR: Harvest House, 2001.

Megan Breedlove. *Chaotic Joy: Finding Abundance in the Messiness of Motherhood.* Ventura, CA: Regal, 2014.

Henry Cloud and John Townsend. *The Mom Factor: Dealing with the Mother You Had, Didn't Have, or Still Contend With.* Grand Rapids, MI: Zondervan, 1996.

Edward M. Hallowell and John J. Ratey. *Driven to Distraction.* New York: Pantheon Books, 1994.

Kate Kelly and Peggy Ramundo. *You Mean I'm Not Lazy, Stupid or Crazy?! The Classic Self-Help Book for Adults with Attention Deficit Disorder.* New York: Scribner, 2006.

Joanne Kraft. *Just Too Busy: Taking Your Family on a Radical Sabbatical.* Kansas City, MO: Beacon Hill Press, 2011.

Jill Savage. *No More Perfect Moms: Learn to Love Your Real Life.* Chicago, IL: Moody, 2013.

Stephanie Shott. *The Making of a Mom: Practical Help for Purposeful Parenting*. Grand Rapids, MI: Revell, 2014.

Jenny Sulpizio. *Confessions of a Wonder Woman Wannabe*. Abilene, TX: Leafwood Publishers, 2013.

Lysa TerKeurst. *Am I Messing Up My Kids? . . . and Other Questions Every Mom Asks*. Eugene, OR: Harvest House, 2010.

Laurie Wallin. *Why Your Weirdness Is Wonderful: Embrace Your Quirks and Live Your Strengths*. Nashville, TN: Abingdon, 2014.

Blogs and Online Resources

The Better Mom, thebettermom.com

Blessed Is She, blessedisshe.net

Finding Joy, findingjoy.net

(in)courage, incourage.me

Life in Grace, lifeingrace.com

Lisa-Jo Baker, lisajobaker.com

The MOB Society, themobsociety.com

The Mom Initiative, themominitiative.com

MomLife Today, momlifetoday.com

Moms Together Facebook group, facebook.com/groups/moms togethergroup

More to Be, moretobe.com

Mothering From Scratch, motheringfromscratch.com

Mothers of Daughters, mothersofdaughters.com

Raising Arrows, raisingarrows.net

Savoring the Everyday Sacred, joyforney.org

This Happy Mom, thishappymom.com

Notes

Chapter 3: What Happens When You Feel Like You're Not a Good Mom?

1. Tammie Head, *Duty or Delight? Knowing Where You Stand with God* (Nashville: LifeWay Press, 2011), 22.
2. "Overcompensation," *Merriam-Webster Online*, www.merriam-webster.com/dictionary/overcompensation.

Chapter 4: Mothering the Way You're Made

1. Phone interview with Laurie Wallin, September 2013.
2. Ibid.
3. Ibid.

Chapter 5: Claiming Your Identity and Aligning Your Priorities

1. Phone interview with Linda Bernson-Tang, July 2013.
2. Elizabeth George, *A Woman After God's Own Heart* (Eugene, OR: Harvest House, 1997), 127.
3. "Margin," *Merriam-Webster Online*, www.merriamwebster.com/dictionary/margin.

Chapter 6: Good News: Your Future Won't Spoil

1. Cindi McMenamin, *When a Woman Discovers Her Dream* (Eugene, OR: Harvest House, 2005), 71–72.

Chapter 7: Working With What Your Mama Gave You

1. Henry Cloud and John Townsend, *The Mom Factor: Dealing with the Mother You Had, Didn't Have, or Still Contend With* (Grand Rapids, MI: Zondervan, 1996), 21.

2. Charles F. Stanley, *Landmines in the Path of the Believer* (Nashville: Thomas Nelson, 2007), 130.

3. Suzanne T. Eller, *The Unburdened Heart: Finding the Freedom of Forgiveness* (Ventura, CA: Regal, 2013), 21.

4. Corrie ten Boom, Elizabeth Sherrill, and John L. Sherrill, *The Hiding Place* (Grand Rapids, MI: Chosen Books, 2006), 247–248.

Chapter 9: Mom Mentors: Turning Rivals to Resources

1. "Passive-aggressive," *Merriam-Webster Online*, www.merriam-webster.com/dictionary/passive-aggressive.

2. Jill Savage, *No More Perfect Moms: Learn to Love Your Real Life* (Chicago: Moody, 2013), 178.

Chapter 11: Valuing Your Role

1. Elizabeth George, *A Mom After God's Own Heart Devotional* (Eugene, OR: Harvest House, 2012), 9.

Chapter 12: Creating Home

1. Marla Cilley, *Sink Reflections: FlyLady's Babystep Guide to Overcoming CHAOS* (New York: Bantam, 2002), 132.

2. Phone interview with Ruth Soukup, October 2013.

Chapter 13: Feeding Your Soul

1. Felix Just, S.J., "Lectionary Statistics," The Catholic Lectionary Website, http://catholic-resources.org/Lectionary/Statistics.htm.

About the Authors

Melinda Means is an author, speaker, and mom blogger at Mothering From Scratch (motheringfromscratch.com), as well as women's ministry director at First Alliance Church in Port Charlotte, Florida. She has been a freelance writer since her daughter was an infant, writing primarily for healthcare publications up until several years ago when her writing focus took a decidedly maternal turn. Her children were simply providing too much humbling and hilarious material to let it go to waste.

Her husband, a high school teacher, has been a long-suffering and enthusiastic supporter of Melinda's journalistic endeavors. She is mother to two highly entertaining teenage children, a daughter and a son.

Kathy Helgemo started out as an English teacher after graduating from Florida State University, moved through various other jobs, and landed in her current role as a freelance writer from home. She is an author, speaker, and blogger at motheringfromscratch.com.

Her husband, Ben, is a pediatrician who can't stop wearing paisley shirts and playing like a kid all day. He faithfully brings her coffee every morning to kickstart her creativity. Kathy mothers four kids ranging in age from middle school to early twenties. With three boys and one girl, she has tackled many issues confronting moms—from breastfeeding to prom.

mothering
from scratch
where encouraging moms is our main dish

Would you like to connect with other women who have read *Mothering From Scratch?*

Visit our blog, motheringfromscratch.com, for more encouragement and support!